Building
Outdoor Play
Structures

Editor: Chris Rich
Art Director: Dana Irwin
Production: Elaine Thompson and Dana Irwin
Illustrations: Don Osby
Photography: Evan Bracken

Library of Congress Cataloging-in-Publication Data
McGuire, Kevin, 1952-
    Building outdoor play structures / Kevin McGuire.
      p. cm.
    "A Sterling/Lark book."
    Includes index.
    ISBN 0-8069-0808-4
    1. Playgrounds--Equipment and supplies--Design and construction.
  2. Outdoor recreation--Equipment and supplies--Design and construction.
  3. Woodwork.   I. Title.
  TT176.M38   1994
  684. 1'8--dc20   94-13704
                                    CIP

10 9 8 7 6 5 4 3 2 1

A Sterling/Lark Book

Published in 1994 by Sterling Publishing Company, Inc.
  387 Park Avenue South, New York, N.Y. 10016

Produced by Altamont Press, Inc.
  50 College Street, Asheville, N.C. 28801

© 1994 by Kevin McGuire

Distributed in Canada by Sterling Publishing, c/o Canadian Manda Group, P.O. Box 920,
  Station U, Toronto, Ontario, Canada M8Z 5P9
Distributed in Great Britain and Europe by Cassell PLC, Villiers House, 41/47 Strand,
  London WC2N 5JE, England
Distributed in Australia by Capricorn Link (Australia) Pty Ltd., P.O. Box 6651,
  Baulkham Hills, Business Centre, NSW 2153, Australia

Printed in Hong Kong by Oceanic Graphic Printing

Sterling ISBN 0-8069-0808-4

Building Outdoor Play Structures

Kevin McGuire

 A Sterling/Lark Book
Sterling Publishing Co., Inc. New York

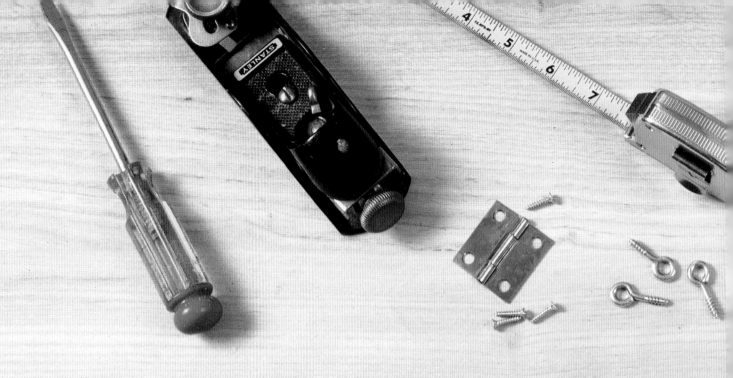

Table of Contents

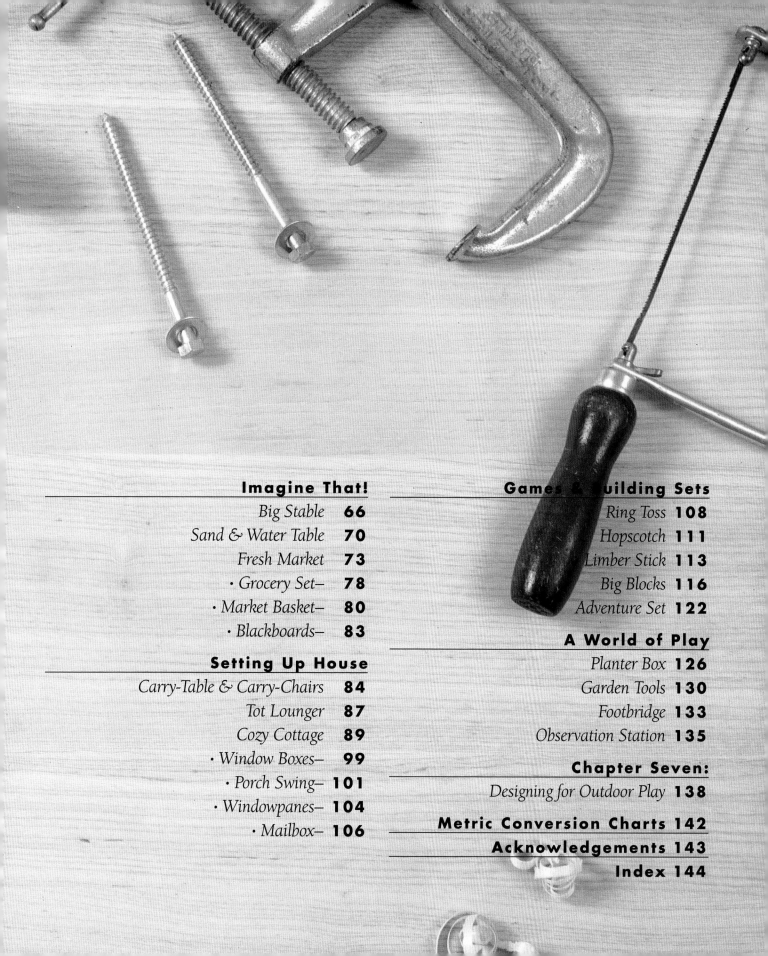

The Ultimate Playground

Imagine, for a moment, coming upon a grassy little hill one late summer day.

This is no high, sloping ridge but a friendly place,

a bump in the landscape softened by thick grasses and dotted with wildflowers.

Being the child you are—and

having nothing better to do—you begin to climb.

As you cross the boulders set into the hill's base, you find a path that circles toward the hilltop above. Along the way, wonderful secrets reveal themselves: primrose and sweet oleander blossoms; a cool and shadowy lair, set into a rocky crevice; broken nutshells and the remains of a beetle or two—signs of a mouse's forgotten feast.

When you reach the top at last, you discover a magical thicket of bulrushes and chinaberry trees, split by an ice-cold rivulet that crosses a bed of sparkling gravel and disappears down the hillside. You fashion a working waterwheel that spins in the current; then you examine a small striped snake hiding at the water's edge.

You climb a tree, and what a view! You can see all the way to India from up here. Then, while you relax in the highest perch you can find, you study those bulrushes down below; they'd make a great hide-out. Next time you come, you'll bring along your best friend.

This little hill is the ultimate playground. With its fantastic variety, its many satisfactions, and its challenges to the imagination, it stands for everything one could wish for in a place for play.

Now, contrast this lovely image with your memory of the old backyard play set, with its creaking swings, sagging monkeybars, and metal slide that turned red hot in the summer sun. Looked like a field of colossal plumbing fixtures, didn't it? And if it was built on an asphalt or concrete landing pad, the results were predictable—ouch!

Times have changed, of course, and play equipment has evolved considerably. Manufacturers now provide more thoughtfully designed play environments, safer by far than their Stone Age counterparts. Schools, in particular, are incorporating more innovative designs for play.

But what about play environments for our backyards and neighborhoods? Creating them can be a real challenge. Catalogues full of expensive play equipment clog our mailboxes. Along with the truly inspired items in them come the ersatz options, from Moon Shoes ("You'll feel like you're at zero gravity!") to accessories for a plastic dream kitchen, including a stove that sizzles and an ice-cube maker that pops out plastic cubes on demand. How to choose? And once these objects are brought home, will they last? Are they worth their cost? And, most important, will the kids really enjoy them?

Commercially available play equipment doesn't always fit well with our vibrant vision of a hillside Shangrila for kids. Yet we're faced with the reality that few children have regular access to comparable outdoor wonders. How can we help our children experience the joys of creative exploration and stretch their capabilities, too?

This book offers thirty answers to that question—thirty projects to build instead of buy. Most of them are well within reach of the beginning woodworker, and they're all designed to keep your kids active, challenged, and excited about being out-of-doors. What's more, their designs incorporate up-to-date information on safety, interest levels, and developmental challenges.

If you're new to the building process, be sure to read chapters 1 through 4, where you'll find valuable information about necessary tools, techniques, and materials. If you're an experienced woodworker, on the other hand, and would like to come up with your own designs for outdoor play projects or adapt the ones within these pages, turn to chapter 7 instead; it's devoted to the challenge of designing outdoor play environments. Chapter 5 offers advice on how to select a project and prepare an appropriate site for it.

While few of us can offer the ultimate playground to our children, we can give them the gift of a place for outdoor play that is full of possibilities for adventure and excitement. Read, build, and enjoy!

Your Workshop

If you're an experienced builder, you're no doubt accustomed to working in your own shop with your own tools—in your own way. The last thing you want is advice that might make your life more complicated. Learning from other builders, however, can contribute to the joy of building and is a process that should never end, so browse through this chapter and those that follow for tips and suggestions to add to your stock of skills.

If you're a beginner, learning to build outdoor projects and equipping yourself to do it properly may seem overwhelming at first, but with the help of this book, you'll soon be part of a true community of builders. Read the information provided and use it to build a solid foundation for your developing skills, adding tips that you pick up from other sources along the way.

WORK SPACE

Most of the work on these projects was done on a pair of sawhorses under the open sky. During inclement weather, when fine work was being done, or when a bench vise was needed, I moved the work inside a workshop just a few steps away. The advantages of building out-of-doors are obvious: there's plenty of room; the bright, even light enhances visibility; and potentially dangerous fumes—by-products of the building process—are better dispersed than they would be in a closed environment. Besides, working outdoors is a special pleasure; it refreshes the spirit and keeps the mind alert.

Of course, working outdoors requires carting tools in and out, and sudden weather changes can mean a scramble to get things under cover, but larger and longer lumber pieces should certainly be cut and prepared outdoors.

Building indoors also has its advantages: tool organization and accessibility; the familiar layout of the work space; and a level floor. Rain or shine, the shop's available, and when the work is finished for the day, a brief straightening up is all that's required. In addition, designing a new project is an indoor activity and is best completed at a separate work station set up for that purpose.

If you're working indoors, a dust-collection and ventilation system is recommended. Consider having this equipment installed by a contractor conversant with such systems. While paper dust masks can provide minimal protection from sawdust inhalation, most are ill fitting and ineffective. A properly fitted respirator is a better alternative and is a necessity when you're working around noxious vapors. Be sure the respirator is rated to be effective against the specific hazard that you're trying to avoid.

Lighting requirements for the various work areas of your shop are similar in many ways to those for the area around a drafting table. For details, see "Setting Up Design Space" on pages 140-141.

Safe power sources are properly grounded receptacles carrying current of sufficient voltage to handle the maximum load that you expect to draw at any given time—plus a generous margin. If you're in doubt about the safety of your shop's electrical system, have it checked by a licensed electrical contractor.

A drop-cord or reel suspended from the ceiling is an ideal source of power for hand-held power tools; it's nearby when you need it, yet out of the way when you don't. High-quality, three-prong extension cords should be checked regularly for wear and should never be used out-of-doors in damp weather.

WORKBENCH AND VISE

The heart of any shop is a workbench that's sturdy enough to support your work pieces and heavy enough to absorb hammer blows without vibrating. To prevent *racking* (the lateral movement of lumber that can turn crosscut sawing into a miserable test of nerves), diagonal cross-bracing and bolted construction are helpful.

Whether you build a bench or buy one, make sure that its working surface is approximately hip height. If you construct a bench, overbuild for strength by bolting or gluing substantial timbers together to form a thick, vibration-free top.

A solid wood "Euro-style" bench usually includes a cast-iron bench vise (with replaceable wooden jaws) or a pair of vises. No matter what style of bench you choose to build or buy, do yourself a favor and make sure that it has a quality vise. They're available through woodworking-supply outlets, catalogues, and advertisements in trade publications. Avoid the narrow-jawed utility vises available at hardware stores; instead, select the widest, heaviest, and highest-quality bench vise that you can find and afford. It will repay you a thousand times over.

ASSEMBLY BENCH

If the workbench is the heart of your shop, an assembly bench is the extra muscle that's helpful when you're ready to assemble the various pieces of a project. While your workbench or a pair of sawhorses and a makeshift

top can serve a similar purpose, a slightly lower table or broad bench is ideal. Depending on how tall you are, a 24" to 30" height should do. The floor or the ground outdoors may be the only possible site for assembly of really large projects, but these surfaces are just too low for smaller projects.

To keep paints, finishes, and solvents from marring the surface of your workbench, use the assembly bench as a support surface when you're working with them. To store finishing materials, install a shelf below the bench top.

STORAGE

Finding storage space for materials and tools is a matter of "build, beg, or borrow." Some shops stack their longer lumber on end against an out-of-the-way wall where it's easy to reach and doesn't require continual restacking. Any method that you choose, however, should be aimed at maintaining the boards in as flat a condition as possible. You'll probably want to build some sort of rack or overhead unit in which to stack the odd materials that you'll accumulate.

While the most common storage devices for small tools may be pegboard wall racks or a few nails on a wall, a better choice is a chest or tool cabinet. The variety of

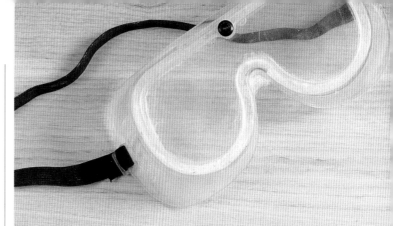

great tool cubbies around is impressive: engineers' chests, with dozens of small flat drawers; salvaged chests-of-drawers, remodeled to suit the builder's needs; intricate custom-built chests made of bubinga and satinwood, with enough stopped dovetails and compound splined-miter joints to make even the diehard cabinetmaker swoon. Whichever make or model you select, consider the chest's volume and division of space.

Rust-inhibitive papers, which discourage rust when they're placed in chests or cabinet drawers, are available through catalogues and are a cheap investment against corrosion. There's no way to prevent corrosion in a damp shop, however, so keep the humidity in your work space under control.

Nothing offers portable tool storage like a leather tool apron; it serves as a walking tool chest and saves hours of wasted time and miles of wasted motion.

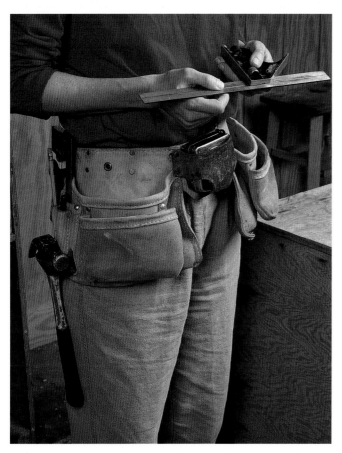

Purchase the best apron that you can afford. To maintain it, empty the pockets regularly and brush away the accumulated sawdust and debris. Apply a bit of leather conditioner now and then. Like all high-quality tools and true friends, a well-made tool apron should last a lifetime.

BUILDING SAFELY

■ A safe shop environment begins with regular cleanup and removal of scraps and other debris. Don't just pile up old rags or restack cutoffs; store scraps properly and dispose of trash where it won't create a fire hazard or get in your way.

■ Never work when you're exhausted or distracted. Research shows a marked correlation between hand injuries and levels of alertness; the results of allowing your concentration to wander can be frightening. Your project isn't going anywhere, so take a nap or catch up on a favorite book and return to the shop when you're fully rested.

■ Remove or roll up loose clothing, take off all jewelry, and tie up your braids if you have them so that nothing except your materials gets near a moving saw blade, drill bit, or other spinning tool. Always wear approved safety glasses when you're working with a tool that's liable to fling debris. Also, don't forget about hearing protection; a quality pair of ear protectors or even ear plugs will reduce damaging power-tool whine to much safer and less unpleasant levels.

■ Tool maintenance should be an automatic weekly and monthly ritual. Check power tools and their cords and plugs for wear and avoid outdoor work in damp weather. The operators' manuals that arrived with your power tools contain complete information that is easily incorporated into your work routines.

CHAPTER TWO

Hand Tools and Accessories

A *tip for beginning builders: Assemble your tool collection gradually, purchasing only those tools required for a particular project.*

LAYOUT AND LEVELING TOOLS

Besides a pencil, a few tools are especially helpful for accurate measuring, marking, and leveling work.

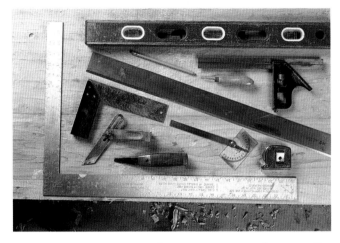

—*Adjustable square.* A knurled screw on this metal-bodied square allows the blade, which is usually 12" long, to be adjusted along its length. The tool is used to mark a board for *rip cuts* (cuts made with the grain of the wood rather than across it), to mark many pieces identically for similar saw cuts, and to mark lines that are square to an edge, a face, or an end.

—*Tape measure.* Don't save pennies on this one. Get a 16'-long, high-quality tape measure with a locking blade and belt clip.

When taking measurements over a few feet in length, get a hand from a friend, as accuracy depends on taking up any slack in the tape. Maintenance is a matter of treating the tape with respect; avoid dropping the case or overstretching the tape itself. If the hook breaks, the tape cracks, or the return mechanism gets cranky, it's time for replacement. With a better-quality tape, it's possible to replace the tape without discarding the case.

—*Try square.* This L-shaped, 90° squaring tool consists of a metal or wood handle that secures a thin metal blade. You'll use it to square across boards before you cut them and to check 90° corners. A square with a blade at least 8" long is more useful than a 6"-long model.

Always keep the square's handle tight against the work that you're squaring. On very wide boards, first square from one edge of the board and then from the other, or use the larger adjustable square or framing square.

—*Framing square.* Grandfather to the try square, this tool is ideal for larger projects that require 90° angles between adjacent surfaces. It's indispensable for squaring across very wide boards and for general layout on plywood. If you purchase a *rafter square*, a cousin to the framing square that has a complicated-looking series of numbers along its *beams* (or faces), you'll be equipped to build a set of roof rafters or a staircase someday. Purchase a steel square instead of an aluminum one; it's less likely to bend when you run over it with the wheelbarrow.

—*Adjustable protractor.* This handy all-metal tool, which is more exact than a standard protractor, adjusts to let you mark any angle from 0° to 180°. It also allows you to read an existing angle from a wood joint and transfer that angle to another location.

—*Sliding bevel.* Like the adjustable protractor, this tool will allow you to transfer an angle from one location to another, but unlike the protractor, it doesn't provide a reading of the angle itself. Often made from exotic woods and trimmed in brass, well-maintained older bevels are truly beautiful.

—*Straightedge.* A 36"-long steel straightedge is useful for checking the alignment of project parts and for laying out full-scale plans on plywood. In many cases, this tool can be replaced by a framing square or level.

—*Two-foot- and four-foot-long levels.* These are necessary for plumbing and leveling larger projects during assembly and for siting them safely for play.

CLAMPS

Project parts must be secured so that they'll stay in one place while you work on them. Several devices will help with this job.

—*C-clamps.* These simple, C-shaped clamps apply considerable pressure to a small area, so they're especially useful for securing aligned project parts for boring. They're available in a range of sizes from 6" and up; the size represents the distance between the jaws when the screw is opened. A single set of 6" C-clamps can improve your work, but a selection in various sizes will prove invaluable.

—*Adjustable clamps.* The great advantage to these clamps, which consist of a long main bar with one fixed jaw and one sliding jaw, is their size; they can be extended across greater distances than any C-clamp can accommodate.

Because of its simple design, this is one tool that you can feel good about buying secondhand. Just be sure that neither the frame nor the screw are bent or twisted and that the screw aligns squarely with the anvil on the upper jaw.

—*Bar and beam clamps.* For securing or gluing together large assemblies such as frames, bar or beam clamps are the way to go. The I-beam section of steel in the bar clamp (or the thickness of the wooden beam in the beam clamp) helps stabilize and flatten the work as well as secure it. Bar clamps are available in lengths up to 6'; beam clamps are limited in size only by the length of the timber from which the beam is made.

To protect clamped wood, insert store-bought clamp pads or small blocks of soft wood between the jaws and your work.

HAMMERS, MALLETS, AND CHISELS

Hammers, mallets, and chisels are available in a bewildering array; each type is best suited for a different purpose. For your play projects, you'll need just a few of these tools.

—*Sixteen-ounce (454 g) claw hammer.* For driving and pulling nails, purchase the best fiberglass-handled hammer you can afford; you'll never use another tool more often. For large projects that require lots of 16d or larger nails, consider buying a 22-ounce (625 g) framing hammer, too. Its extra weight reduces the effort necessary to drive nails, and the checkered face on its head, which offers extra gripping power on the nail heads, helps ensure accurate driving.

—*Nail set.* When it's struck lightly with a hammer, this tool buries a nail's head just below the surface of the wood so that the head can be covered with wood filler when the project is finished. Nail sets come in various sizes to match nails of different sizes.

—*Two-pound (909 g) sledgehammer.* This baby sledge is useful for aligning large project parts such as the timber framing for the Cozy Cottage project (see pages 89-98).

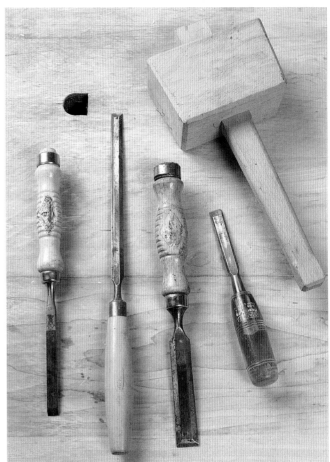

To avoid marring your work, place a piece of scrap wood between the sledge and the timber.

—*Rubber mallet.* Here's your tool for aligning smaller project parts during assembly. Shot-filled composition mallets don't cause the "bounce-back" common to rubber mallets.

—*Bench mallet.* The broad face, light weight, and solid construction of this traditionally styled tool make it ideal for powering chisels of all kinds. Purchase a good-quality mallet from a catalogue or specialty woodworking store.

—*Carpenter's chisel.* Small enough to live in your tool apron, this tool is just right for removing an extra bit of wood here and there. Its steel cap and plastic handle can take a lot of punishment and can be struck with a hammer as well as a mallet. A 3/4"-wide blade is excellent for general work, but get several sizes if you can.

—*Bench chisel.* The hefty size and sturdy construction of this wood-handled chisel make it perfect for removing lots of wood. The thick blade, which is rectangular in section, delivers substantial power when it's struck by a mallet. Get a set of bench chisels in various sizes or put together a set as you can afford it.

—*Firmer chisel.* A good supplemental tool for more refined work, this chisel is differentiated from the bench chisel by its beveled sides. The bevels allow the tool to be worked into tight corners, so firmer chisels are perfect for cleaning waste from mortises.

—*Paring chisel.* This remarkable chisel is never struck with a mallet or hammer; force is delivered to it from your shoulder, through your arm and hand. The tool trims paper-thin sections of wood and eases assembly of ill-fitting project parts.

HANDSAWS

The power that drives larger handsaws such as panel saws, backsaws, and keyhole saws originates in the body and shoulder; straight cuts are made by keeping the shoulder, arm, and hand parallel to the blade. To use the smaller coping saw or fret saw effectively, a smooth sawing action, a light touch, and a well-maintained tool are required.

All saws should be maintained in tiptop shape. Unless you're skilled at sharpening toothed tools, get an experienced saw filer to put that razor-sharp edge on your favorite saw blade. Whichever saw you're using, secure the wood so that it doesn't move while you're working on it and always keep your eye on the line once you start!

Six handsaws were used to build the projects in this book; in a pinch, however, you can get by without the fret saw, the baby of the bunch.

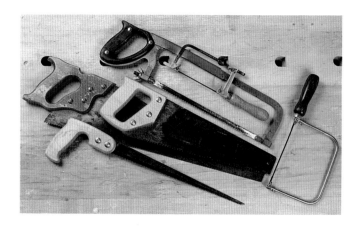

—*Panel saw.* The standard tool for cutting across the grain is a crosscut panel saw. Purchase one that suits your build—and your building needs—keeping in mind that each saw's alternately beveled teeth are sized differently, depending on how fine a cut is desired. For general work, eight teeth per inch is a good choice. If you find yourself doing a lot of ripping, consider investing in a rip saw; its chisel-like teeth are better suited for this purpose than the teeth of a crosscut saw.

As with any saw, keep the teeth sharpened and well away from nails and other hardware. Make sure that the saw screws are tight and avoid bending the blade.

—*Backsaw.* The rectangular blade and the thick back of this saw provide the rigidity necessary for accurate cuts on smaller stock. The fine teeth are ideal for sawing dowels and similar pieces that tend to splinter when they're cut with a panel saw.

—*Miter box.* Used in conjunction with a backsaw, the miter box keeps cuts straight and clean when you're sawing pieces such as dowels. To make a simple miter box, use nails or screws to join three pieces of 3/4" x 3-1/2" x 12" wood so that the edges of one piece are fastened to the faces of the other two to form a "C" shape. Place the base (or center section) of the assembly face down on your work surface. Then make a centered saw-cut through both uprights, exactly perpendicular to the base. Stop cutting just before the saw's teeth reach the base. To use the miter box, place a marked dowel inside the assembly, aligning the mark with the slot that you've cut, and hold the dowel in place against one upright. Insert the saw in the slot and saw down through the dowel.

—*Coping saw.* Indispensable for sawing fine curves, this saw *copes* (or cuts) with a thin, flexible blade, which is secured by two pin holders to a U-shaped frame.

Because the blade can be rotated in the frame, cuts can be made in tight spaces. Replace the slender blade often, and when it's in use, apply pressure to it lightly so that it doesn't break.

—*Fret saw.* Little sister to the coping saw, this tool is used to cut delicate curves on small stock. Its blade is very thin and fine toothed, so light pressure is essential.

—*Keyhole saw.* The pointed blade of this tool can be inserted into a bored hole in order to start interior cuts. Its large teeth can cause serious tear-out on plywood, so use the keyhole saw only for cuts that coping and fret saws can't reach.

—*Hacksaw.* This versatile saw cuts soft steel, brass, and many other metals and materials with ease. Select the proper blade for the job; blades are categorized by the types of material they'll cut.

For maximum cutting power, adjust the tension nuts correctly. Always let the saw do the work; cutting through metal takes time, and forcing the tool to cut faster than it's meant to increases the risk of blade breakage, ruined work, and possible injury.

RASPS

Three rasps were used to smooth rough edges on the projects in *Building Outdoor Play Structures*.

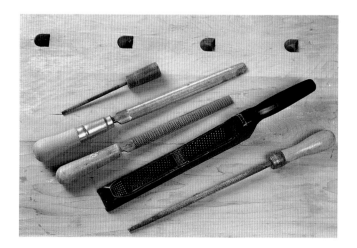

—*Half-round rasps.* These are useful for smoothing flat and concave surfaces. Choose a rasp with a tooth pattern (rough or smooth) that's suited to your work.

—*Round rasps.* Available in sizes ranging from large to small, these tools smooth the interiors of bore holes.

—*Large, flat rasps.* The version shown in the photograph works well for smoothing complex shapes. Its open, smoothing surface allows it to cut especially quickly.

HAND DRILLS, BITS, AND SCREWDRIVERS

For boring holes and for driving screws the easy way, you'll need the hand tools described in this section.

—*Twist drill.* The twist drill bores holes more slowly than a power drill, but it gets the job done all the same, and its geared crank is surprisingly efficient for boring small holes. Use brad-point bits or standard, double-fluted twist-drill bits; the chuck holds bits up to about 1/4" in diameter. (For descriptions of these bits, see page 21.)

To avoid *skating* (the tendency of the bit's tip to slip before it enters the wood's surface), use a nail to dimple the spot where you plan to bore.

—*Brace and bit.* For your toughest drilling jobs, this workhorse combines hefty construction and efficient design to send plenty of power through specially designed bits. The square-shanked bits clamp solidly into the chuck, and the screw-tip on each bit encourages steady, nearly effortless boring without skating. Bits are graduated in size by sixteenths of an inch; the smallest is 1/4". For large holes, use an expansion bit, which adjusts from around 7/8" up to around 1-1/2".

Quality braces and bit sets can be expensive; for bargains, try tool auctions, flea markets, or the classified ads in your local newspaper.

—*Screwdrivers.* Most of the screws called for in our projects are bugle-headed, Phillips-drive screws, with an X-shaped slot in their heads. Though these screws can be driven with a power-drive bit (see page 21), there are two good reasons for having on hand both flat-bladed and Phillips-head screwdrivers in a variety of sizes and lengths.

You'll use your Phillips-head screwdrivers to adjust the screws that you've inserted with a drive bit. The tips of these screwdrivers are sized to fit different-size screws; No. 2 tips work well for medium-sized Nos. 6, 8, and 10 screws, while Nos. 1 and 3 tips work for smaller and larger screw sizes, respectively.

Your flat-bladed screwdrivers will come in handy when you can't find Phillips-drive screws in the sizes or lengths that you need and you have to use straight-slotted flathead screws as substitutes.

Restore worn *flats* (or working ends) by touching them up with a pocket stone (see pages 21-22).

FIVE TOOLS FOR AN EFFICIENT SHOP

Every builder has a few favorite tools. Listed in this section are five time-savers that can help to make designing and building a real pleasure.

—*Marking knife.* For marking crisp layouts on all types of stock, nothing can beat this knife, not even the gnarled pencil stub that you've hoarded forever. The marking knife is used in tandem with squares, sliding bevels, and the like. While any small knife will work in a pinch, the best knives have a flat-edged blade for scribing along a metal-edged tool.

This knife can also make an exact reference mark on damp or dark lumber, a task that pencil toters find especially aggravating. Because most layouts are used as guidelines for sawing, chiseling, or driving nails or screws, the slight impressions left by the blade are generally removed by the subsequent use of tools and insertion of hardware. Visible knife lines on heirloom furniture and timber frame structures, however, are considered signs of authenticity and meticulous craftsmanship.

—*Saw square.* Repetitive crosscuts made with this tool and a sharp-bladed circular saw can rival in accuracy and efficiency those made with a table saw. Adjustable metal saw squares, available commercially, are very handy for making miter cuts and 90° cuts, too.

—*Bench hook.* For trimming dowels or other small, oddly shaped pieces of stock to length, there's nothing like a

bench hook to help you hold the material as you cut.

—*Pocket engineer's adjustable try square.* This palm-sized square, available from engineering-supply stores and through catalogues, is more comfortable to hold than its larger cousin; and because it's usually manufactured to more exacting standards, it gives consistently accurate results. Use it for laying out rip cuts, squaring small stock, and checking your circular-saw blade for 90°.

—*Adjustable spokeshave.* This smoothing tool, a pint-sized cousin to the drawknife, can shape dowel ends, quickly *ease* (or break) an edge and *arris* (the line where edges, ends, or faces meet one another) of almost any solid wood, and soften the arrises of larger shapes when a finely sanded finish isn't necessary. What's more, it's easy to master. Depth setting is easier with models that have knurled adjustment screws.

CHAPTER THREE

Power Tools and Tool Maintenance

POWER TOOLS

In addition to hand tools, just six power tools—all hand-held—were used to build the projects in this book. While certain processes could have been speeded up or made marginally more accurate by using other portable or stationary shop equipment (a biscuit cutter, a table saw, or a drill press, for example), the basic power tools described in this section are efficient and affordable workhorses that will give you accurate results over many years' use.

Safe work habits for power-tool use are similar to those for hand-tool use. Always maintain your power tools in prime condition. Make sure that your power source is adequate; check your owner's manual for specific information about line requirements. Before you begin a project, be certain that your blades and bits are suited for the work at hand and that they're properly installed in your tools.

—*Belt sander.* For removing tool marks, dents, and scratches, nothing beats a belt sander, which is floated back and forth across the work. As a general rule, follow the grain of the wood, and keep in mind that the powerful belt sander requires deft control and a light touch.

Choose a belt sander that accepts standard belt sizes, that is comfortable to grip, and that's powerful enough to stand up to hard work. An amperage rating of 7.5 is a good minimum.

—*Orbital pad sander.* Also known as a finishing sander, this tool removes scratches and marks left by other tools, including the belt sander. Its orbital action

eliminates most of the scratches from your work, leaving the work smooth and ready for finishing.

Sandpaper—Whichever type of sander you use, select sandpaper (in sheets or belts) that is right for the job. Sandpapers for pad sanders include flint, garnet, and aluminum oxide papers; each is named for the type of material that's glued to the paper backing. Flint paper is the least expensive, but it doesn't hold up very well. Garnet paper is both fast cutting and durable. Aluminum oxide paper is the most expensive; it doesn't fill with debris as quickly as garnet paper and smooths rough spots very quickly.

Sheets of sandpaper come in a range of grit sizes. For our projects, you'll need 100-grit sheets for rough sanding and 220-grit sheets for fine sanding. Sanding-belt grit sizes range from very coarse (40- or 60-grit) for your roughest work to fine (120-grit) for work that's ready for pad sanding. To save money, purchase belts by the box.

—*Circular saw.* This versatile cutting tool usually spins a 7-1/4" blade that will cut to a perpendicular

depth of 2-1/4" and a 45° depth of 1-3/4". Many circular saws can be fitted with an optional rip fence, which serves as a guide when you make rip cuts. The fence is adjusted to the desired width of the cut and tightened onto the saw's table by means of a thumbscrew.

The two blades that you'll need for these projects are a carbide-tipped crosscut blade for general work and a finer-toothed, all-steel blade for plywood; the latter will reduce splintering. For efficient sawing, the blade should be adjusted to a depth approximately 1/4" below the surface of the stock that you're cutting.

Observe basic safety rules and the manufacturer's instructions when you use this saw. Wear eye protection and keep everything but your material well clear of the blade.

If there's a trick to sawing a straight line, it's mostly mental! Position yourself securely before starting the saw and use your upper body—including your shoulder, wrist, and hand—to guide and support the saw as it follows the layout line.

While most saw cuts start at an edge of your work, others (typically on plywood) must be started in the interior portion of your stock. These *pocket* (or interior) cuts are made by tipping the saw toward the *toe* (or front

edge) of its table, retracting the blade guard, starting the saw, and then lowering the blade onto the line that you're cutting. To prevent kickback during this type of cut, grip the saw firmly and keep the toe pressed tightly to the work piece. When the saw's table rests flat on the work, continue the cut in a standard manner.

—*Jigsaw.* Also known as a *saber saw*, this tool cuts curves very efficiently. High-quality jigsaws have an orbital blade action, which increases their cutting efficiency by moving the blade forward and backward as well as in a reciprocal (up-and-down) direction. For angled cuts, the tool's small table adjusts to 45°.

A wide variety of jigsaw blades are available for many different materials, including hardwoods, soft-woods, soft metals, and plastic laminates. The triangular flush-cutting blade is especially useful; it permits the tool

to saw flush to a projection. Because all jigsaw blades are fragile, you should always let the saw do the work; avoid exerting undue pressure.

—*Variable-speed reversible (VSR) drill.* A VSR drill with a 3/8" chuck capacity is large enough for most work. Also available in 1/2" capacity and larger sizes, with a hammer feature for drilling holes in masonry and in your wallet, the VSR drill changes in speed and reverses in direction at the touch of a switch.

Boring holes that are straight and true is a matter of experience. Drill guides, which grip the drill in a frame and ensure straight-bored holes, are available, but it's better to learn how to guide your drill by hand.

Drill bits should be carefully matched to the work that you're doing. In the list that follows, you'll find descriptions of the bits used to make our projects:

Young people are often fascinated by tools, materials, and the building process. If the kids in your house express an interest in your shop activities, working together on an outdoor play project can be the perfect opportunity to introduce them to the joys of building.

Using the projects in this book as inspiration, ask your budding builders what they'd like to make. Guide them toward projects that are basic so that you can involve your youngsters from start to finish. This way, tool use, assembly of parts, finishing work, and cleanup can all be presented as parts of a complete process. Let the kids make as many choices on their own as you deem practical, from design changes to color selections; they'll feel most connected to the building process when their choices lead to results they can see for themselves.

Explain the basics of maintaining a safe and clean shop, and the kids will find building less exasperating and more fun. Make saving and recycling scrap wood and other materials a family affair. And, by all means, turn your next visit to the lumberyard or building-supply center into an adventure the kids share with you.

For the most part, safe building techniques for kids are similar to those for adults. Tools are not inherently unsafe, but they can certainly cause injury if they're handled carelessly. Teach your young builders good work habits by explaining how edge tools, extension cords, and the like can be handled safely and efficiently every time they're used.

Kids should be introduced to hand tools first, and, for safety's sake, their early efforts should be closely monitored by adults. One way to ensure that your kids understand how to use tools safely and efficiently is to make different tools available gradually over time. When children exhibit an interest in power tools, start their apprenticeships by teaching them how to use a pad sander or variable-speed drill; provide an extra hand at all times.

Encourage your kids to think through processes carefully before they pick up their tools; they should learn to see each project as a step-by-step sequence. Read through the project steps and tools and materials lists together and talk over any questions that might arise. Taking these steps will help children see building as an orderly process rather than a free-for-all.

Above all, be a friend to your kids when they need advice or a helping hand. Take turns being the "helper," too; give the kids a chance to lead the way now and then—and before you know it, they'll be building on their own!

Phillips-head drive bits—Substitutes for Phillips-head screwdrivers, these bits take the work out of driving multiple screws. Use a No. 2 drive bit for the No. 6 and No. 8 deck screws in these projects.

Plunge router—A router and its bits shape the edges of a project and make the grooves, slots, and notches required by hardware such as hinges. A 1/2"-capacity

Brad-point bits—These are ideal for general boring tasks. Their sharp points prevent skating, and their double-fluted shanks remove debris neatly from the bore hole.

Twist-drill bits—Though they're fine for basic tasks, these bits, which are available in smaller sizes than brad-point bits, are less efficient and clean-boring than brad-points.

Forstner bits—These bits bore exceptionally clean, flat-bottomed holes and are available in a variety of sizes up to 2" in diameter. A set of Forstner bits, however, is an expensive proposition, and finding someone who can sharpen these bits' unusual edges can be tough. A good alternative is the self-feeding bit, which is used in commercial construction and is available individually at quality tool shops.

Countersink bits—These conical bits dish out hollows to match the heads of flathead screws and can be inserted into predrilled holes of any size.

Countersink/pilot bits—These are one-step drill bits designed to bore holes for screw insertion. The tapered shaft on better-quality bits matches the screw's shape neatly, and bits are available for different screw sizes. As a general rule, pieces to be fastened together with screws should be pilot-bored as a unit so that the pilot holes are aligned correctly.

Stop collars—These detachable collars control the depth to which bits can sink and are used in conjunction with brad-point bits, twist-drill bits, or countersink/pilot bits.

plunge router includes adjustable stops, which allow the builder to control the bit depth easily. A fence attachment makes routing parallel to an edge a simple matter.

TOOL MAINTENANCE

Maintaining your hand and power tools in first-rate condition is a necessary, if mundane, part of building. Purchase the materials and tools in the list that follows and get in the habit of using them for regular maintenance. Your efforts will be reflected in high-quality workmanship.

—*Pocket stone.* Quick touch-ups made with a small, flat, medium-grit sharpening stone can increase both the pleasure you derive from your edge tools and the quality of your work. If you choose an oil stone, keep a small

bolts when their flats are too stripped or rounded for wrenches to grip. The needle-nose type is especially helpful for working in close quarters.

—*Slip-joint pliers.* These pliers, which are essential for maintenance tasks around your shop, adjust instantly to grip larger or smaller nuts and bolt heads.

—*Ratchet wrench.* Used to tighten bolts, the reversible ratchet wrench converts the tiresome circular motion required by a standard wrench into a more efficient back-and-forth movement. Shorter travel for the wrench handle means a lot less wear and tear on your arm and hand muscles, too.

Ratchet wrenches are available individually and come with or without *extension arms*—long stems that let you reach deeply recessed bolt heads and that offer more leverage when you're working around cramped assemblies. Graduated sets of *sockets* (the parts that actually grip the bolt heads) are manufactured to fit extension arms that are 1/4", 3/8", and 1/2" thick. The 3/8" thickness is the best size for general work. The ratchet wrench is also essential for tightening the bolt assemblies on some projects in this book.

—*Hex wrench set.* Sets are available in several size ranges. One that includes sizes from 5/64" to 1/4" will answer most of your maintenance needs. Generally, the smaller sets are most useful for adjusting the set screws common to many builder's tools.

ODDS AND ENDS

As you build these projects, you'll find an occasional reference to tools not described in this chapter or the last—tools such as tin snips and planes. If you have a friend who owns them and if you want to save money, you might do better to borrow these tools than buy them. The project instructions will guide you in their use.

A few of the supplies—the ones that you'll need for almost every project—are omitted from the projects' Hardware and Supplies lists. You can safely assume, for example, that you'll need sandpaper and tack rags for almost every project.

squirt-bottle of light- to medium-weight oil with it. When you renew dulled tool edges, don't forget the flats on your screwdrivers (including Phillips-head).

—*Lubricating oil.* Keep a light-weight oil on hand to lubricate hand-tool parts such as clamp heads and screws. Also oil power-tool assemblies, following their manufacturers' instructions when you do.

—*0000 steel wool.* Called *four-ought* for short, this fine-grade steel wool is perfect for removing the tiny bits of glue or debris that sometimes accumulate on tools; it does a good job of removing light rust as well.

—*Flat bastard-cut file.* A flat file with a *bastard-cut* (angled) pattern is perfect for touching up metal-tipped saw blades and removing nicks from chisel blades. Keep in mind, however, that it's easier to maintain the proper bevels on most edge tools when they're sharpened on a water- or oil-lubricated stone.

A file removes metal on the forward stroke only. You'll know you're getting the job done when the file's face encounters a satisfying resistance as it moves across the work piece; it shouldn't slip around aimlessly. When its grooves fill with metal filings, the tool's effectiveness is diminished, so purchase a file card for removing the filings as they accumulate.

—*Triangular bastard-cut file.* Slim and tapered, this file reaches into tight corners and is used wherever delicate filing is needed. For general work, choose a medium length. No matter which size file you use, always pair it with a substantial handle, one that offers the proper grip for maximum control.

—*Locking pliers.* These are used during assembly to hold small hardware pieces securely and to adjust nuts or

CHAPTER FOUR

Materials and Finishes

While all woodworkers use some of the same tools, building for outdoor play differs from other carpentry and shop skills in one critical area— the choice of materials. There's no point in spending hours on a project if its materials will decompose in a single season, and if they're chosen without regard to weather-resistance, they will. Worse still, the projects can become unsafe before showing obvious signs of disrepair. Although the effects of weather-induced rot are unavoidable over time, the right materials can extend the life of your projects significantly.

The cardinal rule in building projects for outdoor play, particularly ones that will remain outdoors all year, is to use materials that are both weather resistant and "play friendly." This isn't as easy as it may seem; some building products made for outdoor use are treated with chemical agents with which people shouldn't come in regular contact! Among these products are creosote-treated timbers, commonly used as crossties in railway construction.

Happily, building materials that have been proven satisfactory for use in play equipment are commonly available. In this section, we'll offer a thumbnail description of each. By checking around your area, you can then determine what's available and affordable.

THE LUMBERYARD

Wood is a favored material for backyard play projects because it is strong, naturally attractive, and "user friendly" for youngsters. A little time spent learning about the distinctive qualities of the various woods available at the lumberyard will mean hours of work saved and money well spent.

Softwoods and Hardwoods

Two large classes of trees produce woods with differing characteristics. Softwoods are fast-growing trees that typically sport needle-like evergreen leaves. Lumber from softwoods is relatively light in weight, economical, and easily worked with basic tools; all three qualities make softwoods ideal for outdoor play projects. Common softwoods include pine, fir, spruce, and cedar.

Hardwoods are slower growing trees, the leaves of which usually drop annually. Hardwoods produce relatively dense woods that generally weigh more and are harder than softwoods. Hardwood densities vary widely, however; alder and poplar are comparable in weight to softwoods, while oak, ash, and maple are higher in density, heavier, and tougher to work with basic tools. With a few exceptions, such as birch dowels, which are made from hardwood lumber, softwoods are the materials of choice for the projects in this book.

The Parts of a Board

The various parts of *dimension lumber* (the uniformly sized boards for sale at building-supply stores) can be accurately described by four terms: *face, edge, arris,* and *end.* Our project instructions make frequent use of these terms in order to keep you—and your lumber pieces—properly oriented while you work on or assemble them.

—*Faces.* These are the wider surfaces found on opposite sides of a board or on all four sides of square-sectioned stock. Faces are either machine planed to a smooth finish at the mill or left coarse-textured for a more rustic appearance.

—*Edges.* These are the narrow sides adjacent to the faces. Edges are machined smooth and parallel to one another and are usually at 90° angles to the faces.

—*Arrises.* These are the junctures between faces and edges or—in the case of square stock—between faces. In less expensive grades of lumber, patches of *wane* (the remains of the rounded exterior of a log) ruin the 90° angle that normally defines the arris. They make layouts and subsequent work more tedious and the resulting assembly less exact.

—*Ends.* You know where the ends are!

Joints

The wooden parts of your projects are joined together in several different ways, depending upon the relative size of the pieces and their positions within the structure. Following is a brief list of common joints and detail cuts.

—*Butt joints.* The simplest of joints is formed when the squared end or face of one part is joined to the end or face of another.

—*Face and edge joints.* Parts fastened with these joints are connected at their two faces or their two edges.

—*Miter joints.* A miter cut is an angle (often 45°) cut across a piece's face or edge. When a pair of miters is fitted together, the joint is called a miter (or mitered) joint.

—*Lap joints.* Two pieces are lapped when their faces or edges cross over one another. A half-lap joint occurs when notches are cut in the face or edge of each part, and the pieces are then fitted together at those notches to create a two-piece assembly that has the thickness of a single piece. In this book, the term *open half-lap* refers to notches cut at either end of a part, and the term *closed half-lap* refers to those cut at some distance from an end. Open half-laps have one cut edge (called a *shoulder*) on one or both joint halves, while closed half-laps have a pair of shoulders on each half.

—*Bevel cuts.* As used in our project instructions, the term *bevel cut* refers to an angled cut (other than a 90° cut) along the length of a piece's edge or face.

—*Chamfer.* This is a "mini-bevel" that creates a "flat" along an arris. Most chamfers are cut at 45°.

Lumber Dimensions

In recent years, dimension lumber has shrunk slightly as load requirements for lumber in the building industry have been cut to the material's maximum load-bearing capacity. A board is now a 2 x 4 or a 1 x 6 in name only; in the building trades, these dimensions are known as *nominal.* The *actual* measurements of a nominal 2 x 4 and 1 x 6 are approximately 1-1/2" x 3-1/2" and 3/4" x 5-1/2", respectively. Before you begin building, familiarize yourself with the differences between nominal and actual measurements. The chart on the opposite page should prove helpful.

Larger, rough-sawed timbers such as cedar 6 x 6s are often dimensioned to their nominal sizes. Also note that boards of the same nominal size can actually vary as much as 1/8" in width or thickness. Lumber lengths, on the other hand, are usually at least as long as their nominal dimensions suggest.

Plywood, as the result of a final sanding at the mill, is also sometimes thinner than its nominal size. Measuring lumber before you buy it will save troublesome errors during assembly.

Softwood Lumber Sizes	
Nominal	*Actual*
1 x 2	3/4" x 1-1/2"
1 x 4	3/4" x 3-1/2"
1 x 6	3/4" x 5-1/2"
1 x 8	3/4" x 7-1/4"
1 x 10	3/4" x 9-1/4"
1 x 12	3/4" x 11-1/4"
2 x 2	1-1/2" x 1-1/2"
2 x 4	1-1/2" x 3-1/2"
2 x 6	1-1/2" x 5-1/2"
2 x 8	1-1/2" x 7-1/4"
2 x 10	1-1/2" x 9-1/4"
2 x 12	1-1/2" x 11-1/4"
4 x 4	3-1/2" x 3-1/2"
4 x 6	3-1/2" x 5-1/2"
6 x 6	5-1/2" x 5-1/2"
8 x 8	7-1/2" x 7-1/2"

Lumber Grades and Defects

Lumber is graded according to industry standards that fairly describe its appearance and the type and relative number of defects in it. Grades typically run from *common*, an inexpensive grade with frequent defects, to *clear*, a more expensive (and nearly defect-free) grade. There is always some variation within grades, however, so for the best possible selection, hand-pick your lumber at the yard. Some supply centers discourage hand-picking, but you deserve your money's worth, so be persistent in your lumber (and lumberyard) selection; make sure you're getting what you've paid for. By the same token, don't select perfect boards for very rough work, where appearance isn't important. A salesperson can help you learn more about the various grades.

Unless you desire a rustic look for a particular project, you'll want to limit the number of defects in the lumber that you purchase. Common defects include:

—*Knots.* Pin knots are small, tight knots located where limbs were once attached to the trunk of a tree. Though they're unavoidable in all but expensive clear grades, they won't affect your project's quality. Loose knots or knotholes, however, should be avoided.

—*Checks.* Splits along the grain can develop rapidly from small *checks* (cracks at the ends of a piece of lumber), rendering an otherwise attractive piece useless.

Reject lumber with significant checking or accept the consequences later on.

—*Wane.* The rounded arrises (or wane) of cheaper lumber grades result when boards are sawed nearest the rounded exterior of the log. To avoid wane, you'll have to spend more money on a better grade.

—*Warpage.* A twisted or bent piece of lumber may make a great pair of snow skis but may prove unworkable when your project calls for a long, straight piece. Site along a board's length to determine its straightness and reject boards that are too warped for your project plans.

—*Stains, grade stamps, and insect holes.* Avoid these if you plan to put your project's best face forward.

Weather Resistance

Weather-resistant wood materials can be divided into two groups: those that are pretreated (usually pressure-treated) with chemical preservatives and those that are naturally resistant to decay. Each group has certain advantages.

—*Pressure-treated lumber.* Pressure-treated woods (often species of pine) have undergone Fluor Chrome Arsenate Phenol (FCAP) treatment (sometimes referred to as Wolman or Osmose salt treatment) or a Chromated Copper Arsenate (CCA) process. Two degrees of treatment are available: a light-density treatment for above-ground use and a heavier-density treatment for below-grade applications. The heavier-density treatment is more resistant to decay.

Always examine treated lumber to be certain that no residues have accumulated at the surface, where they might pose a hazard to children. Wear a close-fitting dust mask whenever you work with pressure-treated woods; doing so is especially important when airborne sawdust is present.

There are two advantages to using pressure-treated lumber (including plywood): its relatively low cost and its availability in a range of dimensions ideal for outdoor play-equipment construction.

—*Untreated decay-resistant lumber.* Of the woods naturally resistant to decay, cedar is the species most appropriate for our projects. Oils in decay-resistant lumber slow the incursion of decay-producing fungi. Beautiful in appearance as well as highly weather-resistant, these woods are more costly than pressure-treated varieties, but many builders are willing to pay the difference for the naturally handsome look of the finished product. Other decay-resistant woods may be available in your area; ask about them at your building-supply store.

Certain dimensions of decay-resistant lumber—cedar 1 x 6s and 1 x 8s, for example—may be sold with one rough-textured face and one smooth face. This offers homebuilders two different textures for siding and other applications. Other dimensions, such as 6 x 6 timbers, may be available only with rough faces. Sanding does little to remove the coarseness, so if a uniform texture is important on all parts of a project, consider carefully before you place your order.

—*Other woods*. Don't be tempted to select fancy woods such as oak and maple and the other woods typically used for furniture and cabinetwork. The greater expansion and contraction across their grain is only worsened by outdoor exposure; checking, splitting, and loose joints are the guaranteed results.

Protecting Untreated Lumber

Certain specialty woods—dowels, for instance—are ideal for project parts but are not available in pretreated form. You'll need to apply a durable finish to all such pieces in any assembly. Protecting these parts is addressed in "Finishing for Keeps" on page 28.

FASTENERS

The nails, screws, nuts, and bolts used for outdoor projects look a lot like the hardware that's used indoors. If

they're to last, however, they must be *galvanized* (a process by which hardware is dipped into, or electroplated with, a rust-inhibiting finish) or otherwise treated to resist the elements. Unprotected hardware such as nickel-plated screws will break down rapidly in the presence of moisture, will succumb to rust, and will eventually fail completely. At best, unprotected metal fasteners will leave long, dark stains down vertical surfaces where moisture is present.

If you can't find galvanized hardware at your building-supply center, try a business that specializes in hardware sales. Try not to settle for unfinished hardware on outdoor projects; it will compromise your project considerably.

—*Phillips-head deck screws*. Most of the screws called for in the Hardware and Supplies lists that accompany our outdoor projects are galvanized No. 8 Phillips-head deck screws. Occasionally, when the screws are inserted in especially thin pieces of wood, No. 6 screws may be more appropriate; your hardware supplier can help you decide which size to use. Available in various sizes and in lengths from about 1" up to 3" and longer, deck screws are best purchased by the box or pound (454 g). Deck screws with a dark finish that blends nicely with pressure-treated woods are now available in some areas.

If you can't find deck screws in the sizes that you need, get flathead wood screws instead, but keep in mind that these substitutes aren't really made for outdoor use.

—*Lag screws*. With their large diameters and hexagonal heads, lag screws are designed to secure parts to solid wood, are tightened with a wrench, and are sold in diameters of 1/4" and larger, in a variety of lengths.

—*Bolts and nuts*. These can be used with standard cut washers or with larger fender washers; the latter provide a greater area of grip and are ideal for use where thinner plywood parts are being secured. The two common types of bolts and nuts are hex-head bolts, with hexagonal caps that are tightened with a wrench, and carriage bolts, with rounded caps that self-tighten as the nut on the opposite end is secured. Both types are sold in 1/4"-diameter and larger sizes and in lengths that begin at 1-1/2" and increase in 1/2" increments.

—*Screw eyes*. These ring-headed screws are available in wire-gauge sizes 3/32" and up. They're installed with slip-joint pliers.

—*Hinges and other specialty hardware*. For descriptions, see the instructions that accompany each project.

GLUES AND CAULKING

Successful gluing requires parts that fit together neatly, the correct amount of glue, and work that is held securely while the joints set up. For outdoor play projects, glue should be used in tandem with other fasteners; glue-joint failure can be a serious problem out-of-doors.

—*Aliphatic resin glue*. Also called *woodworker's yellow glue*, this glue is the standard choice of most woodworkers for many different jobs; it's quick-setting and strong. Because it's not waterproof, however, it's not recommended for long-term fastening in any but the driest of outdoor conditions.

—*Resorcinol resin glue*. Though you can count on this waterproof glue, its higher cost may be a considera-

tion. Used in boat-building, it's an excellent and reliable alternative to yellow glue.

—*Epoxy resin glues.* Both the quick-drying variety and the type that requires a lengthy open time before set-up are extraordinarily strong but are not waterproof. They can also be rather messy, as they must be mixed prior to use.

—*Construction adhesive.* Commonly sold in tubes for use in caulking guns, this flexible, tough adhesive is ideal for gluing large panels such as those in the Tarzanium project. The caulking gun speeds application and provides a neat, "hands-off" method of getting the glue where it belongs.

—*Silicone caulk.* Available in a form that can be painted, silicone caulk can be purchased in several grades of differing quality and cost. Purchase a type and grade recommended for exterior use. Caulk is an efficient gap-filler and waterproofer for long joints such as those on the roof parts of the Cozy Cottage and the panel seams of the Tarzanium.

FINISHING FOR KEEPS

Although even rot-resistant woods eventually deteriorate, applying a protective finish to the surfaces of play projects is an inexpensive and effective way to add years to the projects' lives. To simplify the selection of a proper finish, a review of a few basic terms and products follows:

—*Prep (or preparation) work.* Prep work is a critical part of successful finishing. Fill all cracks and gaps with a quality paste filler, sand all parts thoroughly with the proper-grit sandpaper, and remove the sanding debris with a tack rag or vacuum.

—*Exterior grade.* Finishes classified as exterior grade are specifically recommended for outdoor use and are mixed from ingredients that resist moisture penetration, mildew development, and the effects of exposure to ultraviolet light (or sunlight). If a product doesn't mention mildew resistance on the label, ask your dealer about mixing a mildew-resistant additive into it.

—*Exterior alkyd primer.* A heavy-bodied finish, alkyd primer seals the wood and readies it for painting without raising its grain. Because a base coat improves adhesion and coverage of subsequent layers of more expensive paint, priming saves you both time and money. Note that the word *alkyd* indicates that thinning and brush cleaning will require the use of mineral spirits.

—*Alkyd enamel.* This paint is recommended for our outdoor projects because it's significantly tougher and longer lasting than water-based alternatives. (*Enamel* indicates a finish that's durable to abrasion and wear of all

kinds). While some builders shy away from oil-based products, application and cleanup of latex finishes takes only slightly less time, and the results aren't as gratifying. If you do choose latex finishes, be sure that they're rated for exterior use.

—*Mineral spirits.* This solvent is used to thin alkyd products; follow the usage instructions provided on the can's label.

—*Water sealers and exterior polyurethanes.* Both finishes offer transparent coatings that highlight the grain of the wood. A sealer is easiest to use. Brushed on or wiped on with a rag, it soaks deeply into the grain and offers a good level of protection and a flat finish. At least two coats of sealer are recommended. For a tougher, transparent look, use a brush-on, exterior-grade polyurethane finish instead. This is a high-tech, armor-like coating that builds a noticeable film above the surface of your project. Available in high-gloss and satin (low-gloss) versions, polyurethane is a favorite with builders who enjoy the natural beauty of the wood's appearance. Always follow the directions on the product's label for best results.

—*Reduced VOC finishes.* Volatile organic compounds (VOCs)—the substances that create harmful vapors—have been partially removed from these finishes. Check with your dealer to see if reduced VOC finishes are available in your area.

—*Brushes.* Available in many sizes, types, and quality levels, brushes can determine the quality of your finish work. For the projects in this book, use high-quality 1/2" to 2-1/2" brushes with natural bristles (for alkyd and oil-based applications) or nylon bristles (for latex finishes).

Do your finishing work out-of-doors if possible and stop it altogether when the weather is humid or the temperature drops below 50°F (10°C). Avoid using finishes that have been damaged by poor storage—containers of water-based finishes that have been left to freeze and thaw, for example.

After each coat of finish has dried, sand it lightly and dust the project well to remove the debris before you apply another coat.

The projects in this book were finished with a basic palette of primary and secondary colors, but colors are virtually unlimited these days, so use your imagination. Do remember that certain hues (notably red) are more susceptible than others to fading from light exposure; check with your dealer for optimal choices.

During the cleanup process, avoid the typical wrestling with spirit-soaked rags by cleaning your hands with a cream hand cleaner; your body will thank you.

Making Decisions

SITES

The projects in *Building Outdoor Play Structures* will function well in a wide variety of outdoor locations. They don't require vast backyards or broad open areas; small lots, side yards, or any underused space will do. The Planter Boxes and the Sand & Water Table can be tucked onto the smallest patio or porch, and even the largest project in this book—the Tarzanium—will fit into the average backyard quite comfortably.

When the weather's unpleasant, certain projects (the Fold-Away Hopscotch game, the Balance Beam, and the Big Stable) can do double-duty indoors. And if space is a real problem, just build one or more of the projects that stack, fold, or knock down when playtime is over: the Fresh Market, the Ring Toss, or the Big Blocks, for example.

Ideally, the site that you choose should give your children some sense of privacy but still be close enough to allow adult supervision of all activities. No play structure should be completely out of adult sight for extended periods of time. Even a flat, open yard, however, can be partly screened by setting out an open-work fence, a few shrubs, or a single low-growing tree. If your children help you set out the plants or build the fence, they'll feel an even greater sense of play-space ownership. Select plants that are safe, sturdy, and appropriate for a play area; your nurseryman, a landscaper, or a landscape architect can help you make the right decisions.

If you're building more than one piece of equipment, try to arrange your play area so that projects work well together. A Sand & Water Table placed right next to a climbing structure will not invite the sort of use for which it's intended! By the same token, avoid clustering structures that offer similar activities; kids soon grow weary of repetition. If you have questions about properly siting your play structures, consult a landscape architect or another professional familiar with design safety.

Neighbors with available common space may want to build a grouping of play structures, one that will offer children many opportunities for outdoor play. On-site installation of various projects constructed by neighborhood builders can be a cooperative activity—a celebration of play that involves young and old alike. Spread the word and turn a corner of your neighborhood into a haven for exhilarating play!

SURFACES

Before you start building, take a good look at the surface on which you'd like the completed project to sit. As a general rule, a steep slope (with a fall of more than 1/2" per linear foot) will present siting problems for any project that depends upon a level surface for its stability or is designed for very active physical play. Use a 4'-long level to check grades, as they're difficult to gauge with the eyes alone. Although slight slopes won't interfere with smaller structures, even a minor grade can make the process of leveling large, fixed play structures a real chore. If the surface can't be leveled, select projects that allow safe play in spite of the grade.

A surface that is simply uneven can be improved greatly by spending a little time with a shovel, a mattock, and a wheelbarrow. Make sure that rocks and debris of a size that might cause injury are removed and carted away.

The type of surface upon which you intend to set your play structure may be one that can't be changed. Obviously, asphalt or concrete can't be made safe for children, at least where structures of the climbing and balancing types are concerned. For this unforgiving type of surface, select projects that discourage falls from any significant height and activities such as swinging and climbing.

Asphalt and concrete are perfect surfaces for wheeled toys and projects designed for quieter, fantasy play; the Fresh Market and the Sand & Water Table are good examples. Hard surfaces also offer accessibility to wheelchair-bound individuals.

Grass, while certainly a great improvement over concrete, is unsuitable as a fall-absorbing surface beneath play equipment. It also wears quickly, and the resulting bare spots can be tough on little people. To transform a turf surface into one safer for children, excavate to a depth of 8", extending the excavation a safe distance from any part of a play structure that invites climbing. Remove the sod and soil and fill the excavation with bark nuggets, wood chips, pea gravel, or another friendly

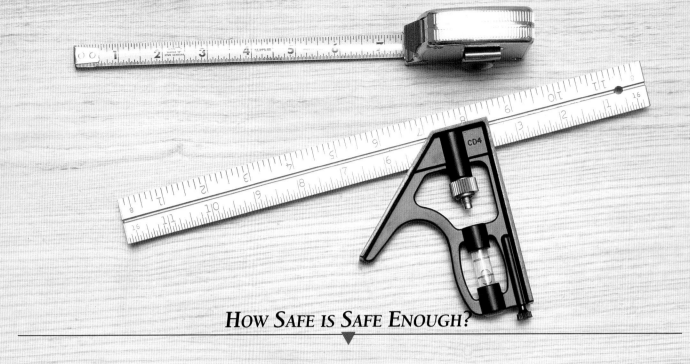

How Safe is Safe Enough?

Risk-taking is part of what play is about. To remove every element of risk from play is to reduce it to an experience that no child will enjoy and from which few children will profit. The question, How safe is safe enough? can be answered by carefully combining the elements of a safe play environment, opportunities for risk-taking, and careful supervision.

A safe play environment is one that meets both the safety guidelines established by agencies of government and the existing standards in the play equipment industry. If you plan to design your own play structures and these guidelines aren't available at your local library, your librarian can help you acquire them by mail. This material is very helpful in answering basic questions about safe play. Add to this information a healthy dose of common sense, and you'll have a worry-free place for play.

Opportunities for risk-taking are chances for kids to stretch their capabilities without risk of serious injury. Ways to test limits should be a part of every play environment and have been built into our projects. The relatively safe risk-taking that they provide offers children the thrills of accomplishment that they might otherwise seek out in unsupervised environments.

Careful supervision means regularly observing your kids at play and knowing when to redirect their play activities toward healthy ends. It can also mean helping new playmates understand the limits and the opportunities of play. Supervision should take the form of caring communication between you and your kids. Let them know that when unsafe situations exist, you'll work with them to discover alternatives for play that are even more exciting!

material. Areas that will sustain frequent impacts (such as the landing pit at the bottom of a slide) should be dug deeper and filled with more material.

Avoid surfacing materials (such as coarse gravel) that are sharp or especially rough and wood waste that includes splintered parts. Municipal ground-wood waste often contains small metal pieces such as nails and sharp tin scraps, so check it carefully before using it.

Keep in mind that wind, rain, decomposition, and active children will eventually scatter and compact whatever cushioning material you use, so check now and then to see that the depth and proper arrangement of the material are safely maintained.

The surfacing material that you use will ultimately depend on what is available and affordable in your community, but a little creative searching can often turn up suitable materials at little or no cost.

PROJECT SELECTION

Choosing a project should be a team effort; by all means, consult with your resident experts—the kids who'll be using it—before you begin to build. If you make a solo decision, you may very well end up with a project that is either too simple or too challenging to catch and hold their interest. If you're curious about the qualities of an ideal play environment, turn to the design section entitled "Including What Kids Need," which you'll find on page 141.

Many of the projects in this book are accessible to kids with special needs. Others, however, will need adjustments, depending upon the particular child's abilities. You are the best judge of a given project's appropriateness for your child. Use these projects as outlines for developing your own designs; for more specific information on design adaptation, consult your local library.

Every project is keyed for a particular age group: look for the key on each one, and keep in mind that these keys reflect average developmental levels. When in doubt, build for the higher age group; your kids won't get any younger!

The projects are also keyed for all-weather or fair-weather use.

✪ The project can be left out-of-doors all the time.

● The project should be brought indoors during inclement weather.

And if you're anxious to save storage space, look for

this last symbol:

🏛 The project knocks down for easy storage.

Also consider the fact that different children enjoy different types of play. A clear distinction can be made, for instance, between action play and quiet play. Quiet corners that offer a nestlike sense of comfort and security are just as important to healthy play as any climbing tower or slide.

Structures such as the Tarzanium provide opportunities for both types of play. The design of this project segregates action play from quiet play so that children in the quiet areas aren't constantly interrupted by the rough-and-tumble activities of children playing in its other areas.

While children often love to test their strength and agility against large fixed structures of all kinds, they also need to manipulate and create playthings of their own and are fascinated by loose parts—objects that can be moved and interchanged easily. Elements that can be sorted, stacked, arranged, and rearranged in endless variations foster wonderfully imaginative play. As an example, watch a child unwrapping a gift; the package's ribbons and wrapping paper may hold more interest than the gift itself.

The Adventure Set project is a multipiece construction set that will provide your kids with the building materials to assemble and organize a project on their own. With its large-scale but easy-to-handle elements, it's a terrific way to encourage truly creative problem-solving. Under the watchful eye of an adult, who should monitor the constructions for safety and lend a hand or a bit of direction when needed, your kids can develop, inhabit, take apart, and recycle their own architectural fantasies.

The Fresh Market project, which includes a variety of small objects, operates on a similar principle to encourage imaginative play. Parts can be added to both these projects and to many others in this book. By using the project plans and instructions as guidelines and by exercising your imagination, you can also create projects in sizes and shapes uniquely suited to your child's wishes. And, by all means, involve your kids in the designing and building processes. For a few pointers on working with your children, see "Building With Kids" on page 20.

Many children love projects that are related to the natural world. The Planter Boxes and the Garden Tools will give them the chance to study the cycles of living plants. Caring attentively for a little backyard box garden is a fine example of learning through play. And what could be more fun than picking and eating your own salad greens or admiring a little ladybug discovered in the box garden and placed in an Observation Station?

CHAPTER SIX

The Projects

It's time to start building! In this chapter, you'll find thirty projects that will sharpen your woodworking skills and excite your child's imagination. The projects are organized into several groups; each group focuses on one broad aspect of play.

The projects in "On the Move" encourage motor-skill development and offer kids opportunities to stretch their growing bodies as well as boost their confidence. "Imagine That!" offers fantasy structures that are designed for imaginative play, alone or in groups. "Setting Up House" offers kid-sized furniture and an heirloom-quality Cozy Cottage too. In "Games & Building Sets," your kids can test their sporting and construction skills with fresh-air games and giant building sets. Finally, "A World of Play" invites children to touch (and be touched by) the natural world.

Select any project that matches both your own skill level and your child's abilities, and whatever you choose to build, enjoy yourself!

 The project knocks down for easy storage.

 The project can be left out-of-doors all the time.

 The project should be brought indoors during inclement weather.

On the Move

BALANCE BEAM

⚙ **3 AND UP** 🏛

The convertible design of this simple balance beam allows young gymnasts to graduate from a wide balancing surface to a narrower and more challenging surface whenever they feel ready.

CUT LIST

| 1 | 1-1/2" x 3-1/2" x 8' | Beam |
| 2 | 1-1/2" x 7-1/4" x 14" | Supports |

HARDWARE AND SUPPLIES

None

SUGGESTED TOOLS

Layout tools
Panel saw
Coping saw
Circular saw
Chisel
Bench mallet

TIP

■ A saw square is recommended for the multiple square cuts required on this project.

INSTRUCTIONS

1. Using your layout tools and circular saw, mark and cut the beam and two supports to length. All saw cuts are 90°.

2. Set the 1-1/2" x 3-1/2" beam face up on your work surface. Measuring 2" from one end, square across the beam and mark it with your pencil. Next, turn the beam 90° so that it rests on edge. Square across the upper edge, continuing from one end of the line you drew previously. Continue until you've squared around both faces and both edges of the beam.

3. Repeat Step 2, but this time measure 3-9/16" from the same end of the beam. Square and mark around both faces and both edges to create a pair of lines 1-9/16" apart.

4. Measuring and marking from the opposite end of the beam, repeat Steps 2 and 3 to make another pair of lines around both faces and both edges.

5. To create the notches in the beam, first set your adjustable square so that the blade extends 1/4" from the handle. Then use the tool to set the depth of the teeth of your circular-saw blade to exactly 1/4".

6. To cut out the notches, position the beam face up and saw squarely along the inside of the first line you marked; all cuts on the beam are made between each set of paired lines. Repeat your saw cuts approximately 3/8" apart between the paired lines, finishing with a square cut on the inside of the second line.

7. Turn the beam 90° so that it rests on edge. Then repeat Step 6. You may find sawing easier if you clamp the beam to your work surface whenever it rests on edge. Continue turning the beam and making saw cuts until both faces and both edges have been notched. Clean up the notches with your mallet and chisel.

8. Repeat these same saw cuts between the other paired lines at the opposite end of the beam, turning the beam as necessary.

9. Set both 1-1/2" x 7-1/4" x 14" supports face up on your work surface and, using the Support Detail as a guide, mark them for sawing.

10. Secure a support piece to your work surface so that the marked edge faces up. Using your panel saw for cuts across the grain and your coping saw for cuts with the grain, saw out the support. Then make the same cuts in the second support.

11. Set the two supports about 89" apart on a flat surface and test-fit the beam's two cutouts in the supports' cutouts. Note that the beam can be positioned in two different ways (with one face up or with one edge up) for two types of balancing play.

12. If the pieces just fit together without sticking, they're ready for sanding. If they don't fit or fit so tightly that they stick when you try to pull them apart, determine where the wood needs trimming and remove the excess wood with a paring chisel.

13. Sand all parts thoroughly. Remove the sanding dust with a tack rag before you assemble the parts for play. If you've used pressure-treated lumber, an applied finish isn't necessary, but suit yourself!

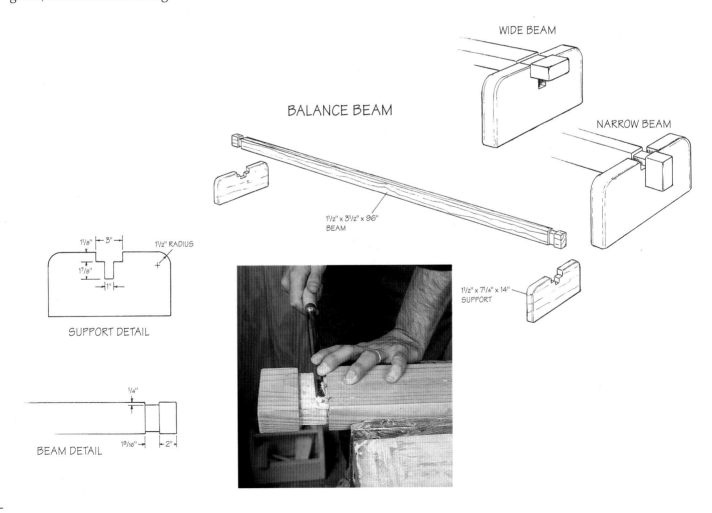

WIDE BEAM

BALANCE BEAM

NARROW BEAM

1¹/₂" x 3¹/₂" x 96"
BEAM

1¹/₂" x 7¹/₄" x 14"
SUPPORT

1¹/₈" ⟵ 3" ⟶
1¹/₂" RADIUS
1⁷/₈"
⟵ 1" ⟶

SUPPORT DETAIL

1/4"
1⁹/₁₆" ⟵ 2" ⟶

BEAM DETAIL

Young acrobats will have a rolling good time on this challenging balance beam. Built around a rotating timber, it includes a grab bar for safe play.

CUT LIST

2	1-1/2" x 3-1/2" x 18"	Short bases
1	1-1/2" x 5-1/2" x 52"	Long base
2	1-1/2" x 3-1/2" x 5-1/2"	End braces
2	1-1/2" x 5-1/2" x 8"	End supports
2	1-1/2" x 3-1/2" x 14-1/2"	Angle braces
2	1-1/2" x 3-1/2" x 34"	Grab bar standards
1	1-1/2" x 1-1/2" x 43-1/4"	Grab bar
1	6" x 6" x 35-1/2"	Log

HARDWARE AND SUPPLIES

2-1/2" deck screws (24)
1-1/4" deck screws (8)
3/4" x 6" lag screws (2)
Washers for lag screws (4)
Water sealer

SUGGESTED TOOLS

Layout tools
No. 2 screwdriver
Bench mallet
Chisel
Round rasp
Panel saw
Adjustable wrench with at least 1" jaw opening
Circular saw
3/8" drill
3/4" brad-point bit
Pilot bits to match screw sizes
No. 2 drive bit
Orbital sander

INSTRUCTIONS

1. Using your layout tools and circular saw, cut to length all the pieces in the Cut List. (Instructions for miter cuts will be given in subsequent steps.) Note that unless your circular saw's depth of cut is 3" or more, you'll need a panel saw to completely sever the 6" x 6" log piece. Label the various parts.

2. Secure the long base face up. Mark two half-lap joints, one at each end; each joint begins 4-3/8" from an end and is 3-1/2" wide and 3/4" deep. To remove the wood from the marked joints, make repeated cuts between each pair of lines with a circular saw set for a 3/4" cutting depth. Then use your chisel and mallet to remove any remaining waste to a depth of 3/4".

3. Cut a similar joint in each of the two short bases; each joint starts 3" from an end, is 5-1/2" wide, and is 3/4" deep.

4. Set the short bases with their joints face down and, using your circular saw with the blade set to 45°, cut a 1/2"-wide chamfer at each upper-end arris on both pieces. Repeat to chamfer the upper-end arrises on the long base but make sure its joints face up when you do.

5. While the joints on the long base are still facing up, test-fit the base-piece joints. (Note that the longer extensions of both short bases should run in the same direction.) Trim the joints' faces with your mallet and chisel until they fit neatly.

6. Bore four equally spaced 1-1/4" holes in the top of each assembled half-lap, spacing the bore holes 3" apart. Then secure each joint with four 1-1/4" deck screws.

7. Cut a 1/2" chamfer at one corner arris of each end brace. Then set the brace pieces on edge, 39-1/2" apart, with their chamfers facing out and down. Set the base assembly, chamfered faces down, onto the two end braces so that the braces are centered along the long base and each end brace's square end is 1-1/2" from the inside edge of a short base.

8. Secure the end braces by driving two 2-1/2" screws through each short base's face and into each end brace.

9. Secure an end support face up for boring. Lay out and bore a 3/4" hole through its face, centered across the face and 3" from an end. Repeat to bore an identical hole in the second end support.

10. Lay out and miter the two corners at the upper end of each end support so that the miters' faces (their angled portions) are each 2" long. Secure each piece well before cutting the miters with your circular saw.

11. Secure the end supports to the base assembly so that one face of each is centered against the square end of an end brace and the square end of each support sits on the chamfered face of a short base. Fasten the parts together with two pairs of 2-1/2" deck screws; drive one pair through each end support's face into the square end of the end brace and drive the other pair through the short base's bottom face (the face without chamfers) into the end support's square end.

12. To attach the grab bar standards and grab bar, first turn the assembly on its side and position each standard on a short base, 1/2" back from the chamfer cut on the base. Drive two 2-1/2" screws through the bottom face of each base and up into the end of each standard. Turn the assembly upright and align the grab bar flush with the end of each standard. Fasten the bar in place by driving two 2-1/2" deck screws through its top face and into each standard.

13. Lay out and cut a 45° miter at each end of each angle brace, as shown in the Brace Detail.

14. Along one miter cut, measure 2-1/2" from a short point and mark the distance on the brace's face. Then square across the face from the mark. Finally, cut the layout line. Repeat to lay out and saw the same miter on the second angle brace.

15. Position the angle braces as shown in the illustration. Secure one end of each brace by driving two 2-1/2" deck screws, "toe-nail" fashion, through the standard. Tie the other end of each brace to an end support by driving a second pair of screws through the outside face of the angle brace (near the "chopped" miter).

16. Set the log piece face up and use your marking gauge and pencil to mark a pair of lines along each face, each 1-3/4" from an arris. Turn and mark all four faces of the log.

17. Set your circular-saw blade at maximum depth; also set it for 45° sawing. Then rip along the layout lines to make the log octagonal in cross section.

18. Secure the log end up. Lay out and bore an 11/16" hole, 4" deep, in the exact center of each end.

19. Use a round rasp to enlarge the 3/4" bore holes in the end supports so that 3/4" lag screws will slip easily through them.

20. Sand all parts of your Log Roll thoroughly, paying particular attention to the grab bar. Then wipe off the sanding debris.

21. Secure the log in position between the two end supports. Insert a lag screw at each end, placing a washer on each side of each end support's bore hole as you assemble the parts. Tighten the lag screws with the adjustable wrench.

22. Finish your Log Roll with two or more coats of water sealer and then call the kids!

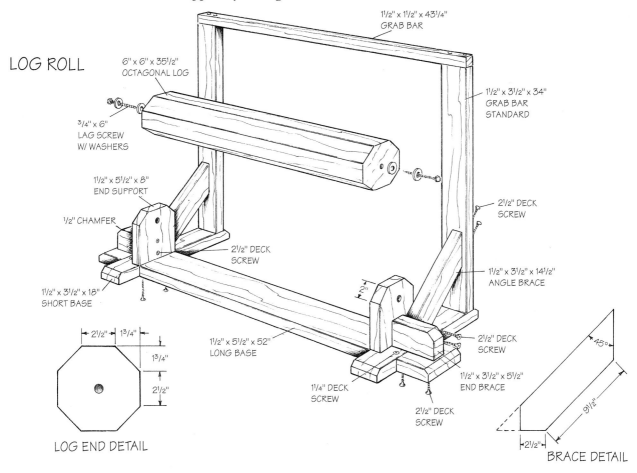

LOG ROLL

1 1/2" x 1 1/2" x 43 1/4"
GRAB BAR

6" x 6" x 35 1/2"
OCTAGONAL LOG

1 1/2" x 3 1/2" x 34"
GRAB BAR
STANDARD

3/4" x 6"
LAG SCREW
W/ WASHERS

1 1/2" x 5 1/2" x 8"
END SUPPORT

1/2" CHAMFER

2 1/2" DECK
SCREW

2 1/2" DECK
SCREW

1 1/2" x 3 1/2" x 14 1/2"
ANGLE BRACE

1 1/2" x 3 1/2" x 18"
SHORT BASE

2 1/2" DECK
SCREW

1 1/2" x 5 1/2" x 52"
LONG BASE

1 1/2" x 3 1/2" x 5 1/2"
END BRACE

1 1/4" DECK
SCREW

2 1/2" DECK
SCREW

LOG END DETAIL

2 1/2" 1 3/4"

1 3/4"

2 1/2"

45°

9 1/2"

2 1/2"

BRACE DETAIL

Active kids will find a thousand and one ways to enjoy this fantastic two-story play tower. The exceptionally sturdy structure itself will thrill your kids, but for the ultimate in play structures, add the related projects that are also shown in the photographs. Instructions for these extras begin on page 48.

CUT LIST

4	1/2" x 48" x 96" plywood	Facings
1	5/8" x 48" x 72" plywood	Platform facing
2	1/2" x 46" x 84" plywood	Window wall facings
4	1-1/2" x 3-1/2" x 73-1/2"	Outside studs
4	1-1/2" x 3-1/2" x 67"	Stud liners
3	1-1/2" x 3-1/2" x 65-1/2"	Inside studs
2	1-1/2" x 3-1/2" x 45"	Bottom plates
2	1-1/2" x 3-1/2" x 42"	Bottom double plates
2	1-1/2" x 3-1/2" x 45"	Top plates
2	1-1/2" x 3-1/2" x 42"	Top double plates
4	3-1/2" x 3-1/2" x 35-1/4"	Peak timbers
2	1-1/2" x 3-1/2" x 14-3/8"	Door lintels
2	1-1/2" x 3-1/2" x 20-1/4"	Blocking
2	3-1/2" x 3-1/2" x 72"	Platform sides
4	1-1/2" x 3-1/2" x 41"	Platform braces
2	1-1/2" x 3-1/2" x 29"	Platform angle braces
2	1-1/2" x 3-1/2" x 86-1/2"	Window wall long braces
4	1-1/2" x 3-1/2" x 39"	Window wall short braces
1	1-1/2" x 1-1/2" x 12'	Window jamb stock
2	1-1/2" x 3-1/2" x 67"	Ladder rails

HARDWARE AND SUPPLIES

1" I.D. x 73-3/4" heavy-walled electrical conduit
  for side rails (4)
1" I.D. x 16" heavy-walled electrical conduit
  for ladder rungs (7)
5/16" x 6-1/2" hex-head bolts (4)
5/16" x 5" hex-head bolt (1)
5/16" hex nuts (5)
5/16" cut washers (10)
5/16" x 4-1/2" lag screws with washers (10)
16d casing nails (1 pound)
6d casing nails (2 pounds)
4d casing nails (1 pound)
Construction adhesive (5 tubes)
Paintable silicone caulk (1 tube)
Exterior alkyd primer
Alkyd enamel paint
Mineral spirits

SUGGESTED TOOLS

Layout tools
Claw hammer
Panel saw
Backsaw
Hacksaw
Flat file
Needle-nose locking pliers
Circular saw
Ratchet wrench with 5/16" socket and extension arm
Jigsaw
3/8" drill
1/8" twist-drill bit
5/16" extension bit
1-1/4" self-feeding bit
Sledgehammer
Router
3/8" rounding-over bit
Belt sander
Orbital sander
Paint roller, roller cover, and roller tray
Paintbrushes
Caulking gun

TIPS

■ The relative complexity of this large project makes it a good choice for more experienced builders. For information on siting it safely, review chapter 5.

■ Cut List measurements serve as indicators of longest dimensions only; more information on mitered ends and other shaping details can be found in the illustrations and in the instruction steps.

■ Labeling all parts will prevent costly mistakes!

■ The major components are held together by 5/16" lag screws or by hex-head bolts. Except when otherwise indicated, all lag screws include a cut washer of matching size, and all bolts include two cut washers and a nut of matching size.

■ Bore-holes for both lag screws and bolts include a 1-1/4"-diameter x 1/2"-deep counterbore and either a 1/4" bore-hole that matches the lag screw's length or a 5/16" through-hole for the bolts. (Bolts also have a second counterbore at their threaded ends.) Counterbores—and threaded hardware of appropriate length—provide a critical safety factor for your children.

- Don't even think about assembling this project yourself, as positioning the large components on your own can be dangerous.
- Should you choose to add any of the optional related projects, the dimensions of certain parts such as the side rails may be altered. Avoid extra work by reviewing the instructions for every add-on before you start to build.

INSTRUCTIONS

1. The Tarzanium is composed of four large panel-like assemblies: the front and back walls, a platform, and a window wall. All four panels are built from framed lumber that is covered with glued-and-nailed plywood facings. Begin by examining the Back Wall Framing illustration. Then use your circular saw to cut the framing parts for the back wall. Arrange them on a flat surface, with their edges face up, for assembly.

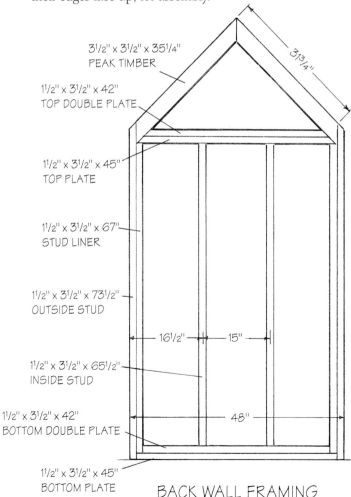

3^1/2" x 3^1/2" x 35^1/4"
PEAK TIMBER

1^1/2" x 3^1/2" x 42"
TOP DOUBLE PLATE

3^1/4"

1^1/2" x 3^1/2" x 45"
TOP PLATE

1^1/2" x 3^1/2" x 67"
STUD LINER

1^1/2" x 3^1/2" x 73^1/2"
OUTSIDE STUD

16^1/2"   15"

1^1/2" x 3^1/2" x 65^1/2"
INSIDE STUD

1^1/2" x 3^1/2" x 42"
BOTTOM DOUBLE PLATE

48"

1^1/2" x 3^1/2" x 45"
BOTTOM PLATE

BACK WALL FRAMING

2. First, fasten two outside studs, two peak timbers, and a bottom plate together, using at least two 16d casing nails at each joint and making sure the top edges of all parts are aligned. Next, toe-nail the top plate into the peak timbers. Then install the two stud liners, the bottom double plate, the inside wall studs, and the top double plate, in that order.

3. Roughly square the assembly by measuring the two diagonals with your tape measure; adjust the framework until both measurements are identical. Then use your caulking gun to run a 3/16"-wide bead of construction adhesive along the center of the top edge of each framing member.

4. Have a friend help you set a 1/2" x 48" x 96" plywood facing onto the assembly so that the worst face "gets the glue." Work carefully, as the glue sets quickly. Align the edges of the facing with the assembly's outside edges and use 6d casing nails to tack down the four corners.

5. To close the gaps between the facing and the framework's edges, walk about on the facing a bit. Then secure it to every edge, using 6d nails spaced approximately 8" apart. Keep the nails at least 3/4" from any edge so that you won't damage your router bit when you round the arrises (see Step 30). To locate hidden framing members, use your tape measure or tap the plywood with your hammer.

6. Use a straightedge or mason's level to lay out the two facing cuts that define the peak at the top of the wall, scribing from the angled framing members below. Then cut the facing. (A plywood blade on your circular saw will reduce the damage to the plywood's face.)

7. Flip the assembly over. Using Steps 3 through 6 as a guide, fasten the second 1/2"-thick plywood facing onto the framework.

8. Caulk all the joints between the facings and the framing members with paintable silicone caulk. Then smooth the caulked joints with your fingertip.

9. Bore several 5/16" through-holes into the wall's bottom so that any rainwater that manages to get inside the assembly will drain from the three enclosed spaces.

10. Using the Front Wall Framing illustration on the next page as a guide, cut and assemble the front wall parts to form a second panel. Note that the differing layouts for the two walls accommodate different hole-boring patterns in later steps. To ensure accurate alignment, scribe the door cutout directly from the framework onto each plywood facing. Cut the facings before gluing them in place.

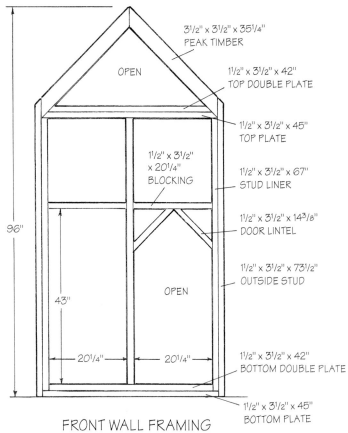

3¹/₂" x 3¹/₂" x 35¹/₄"
PEAK TIMBER

1¹/₂" x 3¹/₂" x 42"
TOP DOUBLE PLATE

1¹/₂" x 3¹/₂" x 45"
TOP PLATE

1¹/₂" x 3¹/₂"
x 20¹/₄"
BLOCKING

1¹/₂" x 3¹/₂" x 67"
STUD LINER

1¹/₂" x 3¹/₂" x 14³/₈"
DOOR LINTEL

1¹/₂" x 3¹/₂" x 73¹/₂"
OUTSIDE STUD

1¹/₂" x 3¹/₂" x 42"
BOTTOM DOUBLE PLATE

1¹/₂" x 3¹/₂" x 45"
BOTTOM PLATE

OPEN

OPEN

96"

43"

20¹/₄"   20¹/₄"

FRONT WALL FRAMING

11. Refer to the Platform Framing illustration. Note the notched, 90° cutout on one end; this opening allows youngsters to climb up the ladder to the platform. The platform panel has a single 5/8" plywood facing; its bottom is left open. Cut and assemble the platform as indicated.

PLATFORM FRAMING

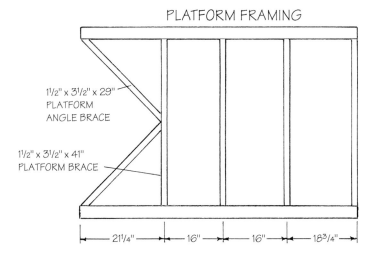

1¹/₂" x 3¹/₂" x 29"
PLATFORM
ANGLE BRACE

1¹/₂" x 3¹/₂" x 41"
PLATFORM BRACE

21¹/₄"   16"   16"   18³/₄"

12. The last panel—the window wall—is located diagonally between the front and back walls; it supports the platform and ties the whole together. Its construction differs from the three previous panels in several respects. Note in the Window Wall Framing illustration that the framing members are toe-nailed edge-to-edge (rather than in typical framing fashion) to form a thinner panel. The two plywood facings have matched cutouts in three places, and the cutouts' edges are lined with 1-1/2" x 1-1/2" pieces called *jambs,* which are scribed to fit each opening. Also note that the 46" plywood ends are held back 3/4" from the 46" ends of the framework and that these framework ends (but not the plywood facings) are beveled to 33°.

13. Begin by toe-nailing the four short braces to a pair of long braces, as shown in the illustration. At each corner, the end of a long brace should be square with the outside edge of a short brace. (Keep all nails at least 2" away from the framework's ends to avoid striking them with your circular-saw blade when you make the bevel cuts in the next steps.)

14. Position the framework safely above the floor for sawing. Next, use a pencil and your adjustable square set for 1" to draw a line along the face of one 46" end of the framework. Then, with your circular-saw table set to 33 degrees, cut the line from edge to edge of the framework. (The saw blade should tilt toward the outermost edge of the framework.)

15. Carefully turn the framework over onto its opposite side, and repeat Step 14 to bevel the second 46" edge.

16. To reduce chipping when you cut the window openings, set the window-wall facing with its best face down. (Bear in mind that because the piece is upside down, the window layout will be reversed from left-to-right.) Carefully lay out the three window openings, as shown in the Window Wall Framing illustration.

17. Using the pocket-cut technique described on page 19, cut as much of each straight layout line as you can. Then finish sawing the uncut portions with your jigsaw.

18. Set the window wall's framework face up so that the miter cut on your right faces the floor and the miter cut on your left faces up. The facing's triangular window opening should point toward the long top edge of the facing, and that edge of the facing should align with the framework's long edge farthest from you. As with previous panels, glue and nail the facing onto the squared assembly, but allow a 3/4" margin between each 46" plywood edge and the 46" miter cuts at either end. Use 4d casing nails, spaced 8" apart, for fastening.

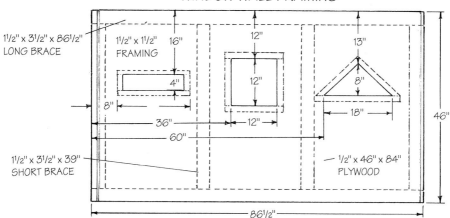

1¹/₂" x 3¹/₂" x 86¹/₂"
LONG BRACE

1¹/₂" x 1¹/₂"
FRAMING

16"

4"

8"

12"

12"

13"

8"

18"

46"

36"

60"

12"

1¹/₂" x 3¹/₂" x 39"
SHORT BRACE

¹/₂" x 46" x 84"
PLYWOOD

86¹/₂"

19. Using the illustration to help you determine where each window jamb fits and the window openings themselves to determine exact lengths and angles, scribe and cut the 1-1/2" x 1-1/2" window-jamb stock. To fasten the jambs in place, drive 4d nails through the plywood's exterior face and into the jambs.

20. Set the second window-wall facing with its best side down on the floor. Then position the framework's braces on it so that there is a 3/4" margin at either end of the plywood. Align the long edges of the plywood with the framework. With your pencil, scribe the window openings from the existing assembly onto the second plywood facing.

21. Remove the plywood facing and cut out the window openings as before.

22. Flip the window-wall assembly over. Then glue and nail the second facing onto it, aligning the parts carefully before you do.

23. With your router setup, round the window openings' arrises on both sides. Also round the four 46" ends of the plywood facings, but avoid rounding the beveled ends of the window wall.

24. Careful layout of boring patterns in the next few steps will ensure accurate assembly later on! First, refer to the Assembly illustration on the next page. Note that the front and back walls are secured to the platform by a capture-nut system, which is described at the end of this step. Bore four 1-1/4" x 2"-deep holes into the platform side pieces' outermost faces; center each hole across the face's width, 2-1/2" from each end of each side piece. Through the face of the front and back facings, 1-1/8" from each wall's plywood edges and 47-3/4" from each wall's bottom edge, bore 1-1/4"-diameter x 1/2"-deep counterbores, one at each corner. (Note that these 1/2"-deep counter-

bores run perpendicular to the 2"-deep bore holes.) After you assemble and align the components, you'll bore a 5/16" through-hole through each counterbore's center (see Step 34); this hole will pierce the capture-nut bore hole that runs perpendicular to it. Then you'll insert washers and nuts into the capture-nut holes in the side pieces and tighten them onto bolts inserted through the walls.

25. Bore a fifth 1/2"-deep counterbore half-way between the two counterbores on the front wall. (In Step 34, you'll bore a 5/16" through-hole through this counterbore and through the outermost 41" short brace of the platform. You'll then make an identical counterbore on the inside face of the short brace, centering it over the 5/16" bore hole. This counterbore will receive the washer and nut at the threaded end of the center bolt.)

26. To secure each end of the window wall, make three 1-1/4" x 1/2"-deep counterbored holes in each wall's outside face (see the Assembly illustration). Note that these holes are located near the left-hand edge of both the front and the back facings. Center them 1-1/8" from each wall's outer plywood edge and 2", 23", and 44" from the bottom of each wall. Complete the six bore holes by boring a 5/16" through-hole in the center of each counterbore.

27. In the front and back walls' inside facings, bore the eight 1-1/4" x 1" deep holes that will secure the metal side rails. Center these holes 2" from the facing's long inside edge and 61-3/4" and 71" from the bottom edge of the wall.

28. The ladder will be secured to the back wall's inside facing by four 5/16" x 4-1/2" lag screws with washers, counterbored 1/2" and through-bored 5/16". Locate the two top counterbores 65" from the wall's bottom edge, 16-1/2" and 31-1/2" from the left-hand edge. Space the

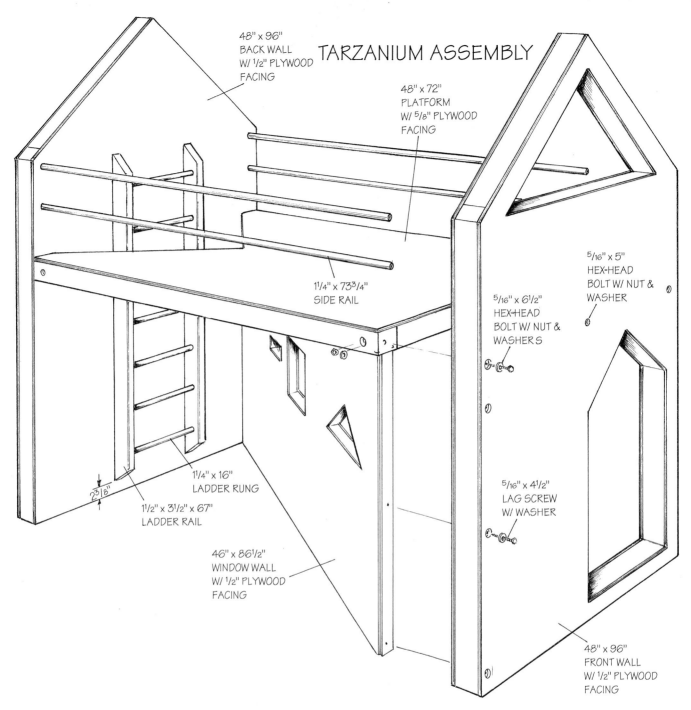

TARZANIUM ASSEMBLY

48" x 96"
BACK WALL
W/ 1/2" PLYWOOD
FACING

48" x 72"
PLATFORM
W/ 5/8" PLYWOOD
FACING

1 1/4" x 73 3/4"
SIDE RAIL

5/16" x 5"
HEX-HEAD
BOLT W/ NUT &
WASHER

5/16" x 6 1/2"
HEX-HEAD
BOLT W/ NUT &
WASHERS

1 1/4" x 16"
LADDER RUNG

2 3/8"

1 1/2" x 3 1/2" x 67"
LADDER RAIL

5/16" x 4 1/2"
LAG SCREW
W/ WASHER

46" x 86 1/2"
WINDOW WALL
W/ 1/2" PLYWOOD
FACING

48" x 96"
FRONT WALL
W/ 1/2" PLYWOOD
FACING

two bottom counterbores the same distances from the plywood edge but locate them 8" from the bottom.

29. Use your hacksaw to cut the four side rails to length and ease their rough ends with your file.

30. To prevent splinters, use your router setup to round all arrises on the front and back wall panels and on the platform. Then thoroughly sand all parts of the four large assemblies. A belt sander is especially useful for smoothing the large solid-wood surface areas. Using 220-grit sandpaper for a smooth finish, complete the sanding with an orbital sander or by hand. Wipe the assemblies clean with a tack cloth.

31. Paint the four large assemblies in your choice of exterior alkyd enamel colors, priming carefully with exterior alkyd primer beforehand. (Using a roller will speed paint application considerably.) For a rock-hard finish, allow each coat to dry thoroughly before recoating.

32. You'll need a hand with the next few steps! Begin by moving the four painted assemblies and the mounting tools and hardware for them to the location where the

Tarzanium will be erected. After you and your helper have reviewed the Assembly illustration together, stand the back wall upright on a flat surface. Have your helper set the window wall upright, with the beveled 46" edge that's nearest to the rectangular window fitted against the back wall's inside facing. The window-wall edge should cover the three 5/16" through-holes, and the point of its bevel should align exactly with the facing's edge. Next, use your claw hammer to tap a 5/16" x 4-1/2" lag screw with washer into each hole and to start each lag screw into the beveled edge of the window wall. Then use your ratchet wrench and 5/16" socket to tighten the lag screws in place.

33. Repeat Step 32 to fasten the front wall to the opposite end of the window wall. As you do so, insert the four side rails so that their ends are captured in the eight 1-1/4" bore holes in the front and back walls' inside facings. Tighten the three lag screws securely. (If the side rails turn in their holes, they may be hazardous for your youngsters; see Step 40 for tips on securing them in place.)

34. Carefully set the platform assembly onto the window wall's top edge. Have your helper balance it while you set up for boring 5/16" through-holes into the five counterbores you made in Steps 24 and 25. First, use your tape measure to mark 46" from the bottom of the front and back walls' outside studs; align the platform's bottom corners at these marks. Then bore through-holes into the five counterbores, making sure to bore as straight as possible so that the drill bit pierces each capture-nut bore hole cleanly. (If you're now out of reach of a power source, you can bore the through-holes by chucking the 5/16" extension bit into a twist drill. It's slow going, but it will get the job done!) Bore a 1-1/4" x 1/2"-deep counterbore centered on the 5/16" through-hole in the center of the short brace's inside face.

35. Tap a 5/16" x 6-1/2" bolt with washer into each corner through-hole. Then tighten a washer and nut onto the threaded end in the capture-nut bore hole; use your locking pliers to grip the nut and your ratchet wrench to tighten the bolt. (If you can't start the nuts onto the threaded ends because the cut washers hold the nuts away from the bolts' ends, bend the washers slightly in their middles so that they match the curved interiors of the capture-nut bore holes more closely.)

36. To secure the front wall to the platform's short brace, tighten the 5/16" x 5" bolt through the front wall's center through-hole with two washers and a nut.

37. Cut the two ladder rails as shown in the Ladder Detail so that the long points of the 45° miters are 67" apart. Then lay out the pattern for the 1-1/4" x 3/4"-deep bore holes on the rails' inside faces, centering each hole 1-1/4" from each rail's front edge.

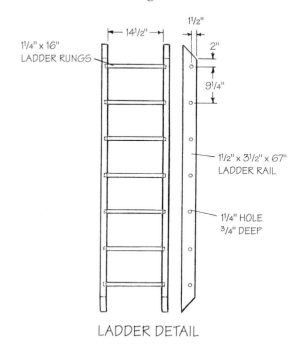

LADDER DETAIL

38. Round all arrises of the ladder rails except for the two back edges—the ones between the miters' long points. Sand the rails and then prime and paint them to your liking.

39. Cut the seven ladder rungs to length and ease their ends with a hacksaw.

40. Insert the rungs into the paired bore holes, using a two-pound (909 g) sledgehammer and wood block if necessary. If the rungs turn in their bore holes, secure each one by first using a twist drill to bore a 1/8" x 2"-deep hole into the ladder's front edge so that the bit pierces both curved walls of the rung. Then drive a 16d casing nail through the hole to pin the rung in place. Repeat at every rung location.

41. Have your helper hold the square edges of the rails firmly against the back wall's inside facing so that the long points on the rails are exactly 2-3/8" above the wall's bottom edge and the ladder is exactly centered across the inside facing's width. Tap the four lag screws with washers through the holes and start them into the ladder rails. Then tighten them with your ratchet wrench. Now, go find a glass of lemonade and a nice shade tree—you've earned them!

G y m

This incredible combination of ropes and monkey bars will thrill your young gymnasts while it encourages the healthy development of their growing bodies. The climbers' creative antics will delight adults, too.

CUT LIST

2	3-1/2" x 3-1/2" x 80"	Top and bottom timbers (H and I)
1	3-1/2" x 3-1/2" x 47-1/2"	Middle timber (G)
2	3-1/2" x 3-1/2" x 44"	Inside short timbers (E and F)
2	3-1/2" x 3-1/2" x 44"	Outside short timbers (A and B)
2	3-1/2" x 3-1/2" x 51"	Outside long timbers (C and D)
2	3-1/2" x 3-1/2" x 21-1/2"	Angle braces

HARDWARE AND SUPPLIES

1/4" x 6" hex-head bolts (28)
1/4" cut washers (56)
1/4" nuts (28)
1-1/4" x 46" heavy-wall electrical conduit (4)
23' of 3/4" sisal rope
16d casing nails (1 pound)
Exterior alkyd primer
Alkyd enamel paint
Mineral spirits
Plastic tape

SUGGESTED TOOLS

Layout tools
Claw hammer
2-pound sledgehammer
Hacksaw
Needle-nose locking pliers
Half-round rasp
Flat file
Ratchet wrench with 7/16" socket and extension arm
Circular saw
3/8" drill
1/4" extension bit
1" self-feeding bit
1-1/4" self-feeding bit
Router
3/8" rounding-over bit
Belt sander
Orbital sander
Paint roller, roller cover, and roller tray
Paintbrushes in your choice of sizes

TIPS

- This project appears complex at first glance, but its unusual shape is nothing more than a large, open cube turned up onto one arris and secured to the Tarzanium by two long timbers.
- Note that keys are provided for the Timber Layout and Timber Identification illustrations.
- If the heavy-wall conduit that you purchase has an outside diameter larger than 1-1/4", you'll need a larger self-feeding bit.
- The Gym and Tarzanium must be sited on a level grade. If your site isn't reasonably level, refer to pages 29 and 31.
- The Gym is heavy; you'll need help assembling and moving it.

INSTRUCTIONS

1. The Gym's nine timbers are fastened together using the capture-nut system described in Step 24 of the Tarzanium project. Review this system and study the Connector Detail on page 52 before beginning the Gym. Then lay out and cut the timbers to length, flipping each timber as necessary to complete the cuts. (Don't cut the two angle braces just yet.)

2. Using the Timber Layout illustrations, which provide boring patterns for each piece, lay out the locations for the counterbores (C) and capture-nut bore holes (N) in the timbers. Then bore the holes, using the 1" self-feeding bit to bore the counterbores, the 1-1/4" self-feeding bit to bore the capture-nut holes, and the 1/4" extension bit to bore the through-holes (T) between the counterbores and capture-nut holes. The through-holes should be bored with adjacent timbers secured in position, a pair at a time, placed face up on a flat surface such as the floor or a piece of plywood. Note that the six counterbored holes (A) in the top and bottom timbers, which will be bored in Steps 17 and 18, are bored diagonally from arris-to-arris.

3. Lay out the locations on the timbers for the eight 1-1/4" x 1-1/8"-deep bore holes (B) for the monkey bars and the six 1" through-bores (R) for the ropes. (Note that the two holes for the vertically mounted rope are bored diagonally through the top and bottom timbers, from one arris to the opposite arris.) Bore the holes, using the appropriate bits.

4. Cut a 1/2"-wide chamfer around all four arrises of one end of the top timber and one end of the bottom timber, making them on the ends farthest from the rope

TIMBER LAYOUT

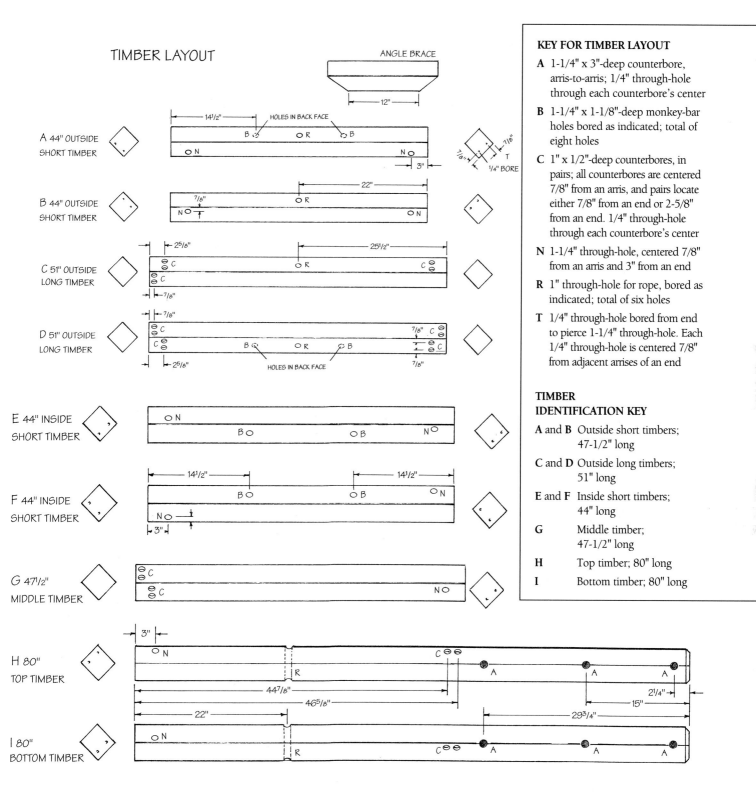

ANGLE BRACE

12"

A 44" OUTSIDE SHORT TIMBER

14¹/₂"   HOLES IN BACK FACE
B   R   B
N   N
3"

B 44" OUTSIDE SHORT TIMBER

22"
R
⁷/₈"   N   N

7/8"   T
7/8"   1/4" BORE

C 51" OUTSIDE LONG TIMBER

2⁵/₈"   25¹/₂"
C   R   C
C
⁷/₈"

D 51" OUTSIDE LONG TIMBER

⁷/₈"   ⁷/₈"   C
C
C   B   R   B   C
2⁵/₈"   HOLES IN BACK FACE   ⁷/₈"

E 44" INSIDE SHORT TIMBER

N
B   B   N

F 44" INSIDE SHORT TIMBER

14¹/₂"   14¹/₂"
B   B   N
N
3"

G 47¹/₂" MIDDLE TIMBER

C
C   N

H 80" TOP TIMBER

3"
N
R
C   A   A   A
44⁷/₈"
46⁵/₈"
2¹/₄"
15"

I 80" BOTTOM TIMBER

N
R
C   A   A   A
22"
29³/₄"

holes. To make each chamfer, set the circular-saw blade at 45° and cut a layout line scribed on each face exactly 3/8" from the end's arris. ("1/2-wide chamfer" describes the width of the finished chamfer's cut surface.)

5. Get some help with the next few steps! Begin the Gym's assembly by tightening the capture-nut hardware into the four outside timbers (A, B, C, and D) to form a square frame. Then, while your helper holds each one in position, attach the middle, top, and bottom timbers (G, H, and I) to the assembly.

TIMBER IDENTIFICATION

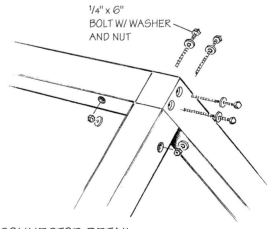

6. With your hacksaw, cut the electrical conduit for the monkey bars into four 46" lengths; then ease their cut edges with a file.

7. Set the assembly so that the square frame rests flat on the ground and the top, bottom, and middle timbers point upward. Install the ends of the monkey bars into the four holes on the square frame, using the sledgehammer and a block of wood to bump them a bit if the fit is tight.

8. Bolt the two inside short timbers (E and F) in place, securing them onto the ends of the monkey bars as well.

9. The angle braces are each cut with a pair of 45° mitered ends. (As indicated in the illustration, each pair of miters is located on the same face of each brace.) Lay out and saw the miters so that the distance between their short points is 12".

10. Position the angle braces between the square-framed end of the Gym and the top and bottom timbers. Align the joints' edges carefully and use four 16d casing nails to secure each miter joint.

1/4" x 6" BOLT W/ WASHER AND NUT

CONNECTOR DETAIL

11. With your router setup, round every arris on the Gym. Where the Gym's arrangement of timbers prevents the router from reaching an arris, round it with your rasp.

12. Using your belt and orbital sanders, thoroughly sand the project; sand by hand wherever power tools can't reach. Remove the sanding debris with a tack rag.

13. Prime and paint the Gym.

14. Cut the rope into three pieces: two 7' pieces for the square frame's crossed ropes and one 9' piece for the vertical rope.

15. Install the ropes in the Gym's 1" bore holes as illustrated, knotting them every 7" or so to provide grips for little hands. Make the knot at the juncture of the two crossed ropes by knotting one rope around the other. Tighten the two crossed ropes as much as possible between the square frame's bore holes, but leave several inches of slack in the vertical rope or the knotted end at the bottom will hold the Gym's bottom timber off the ground and create an unsteady assembly. To prevent the ropes' ends from unraveling, wind several turns of plastic tape around each one.

16. With your helpers, position the Gym against the Tarzanium so that the faces of the top and bottom timbers fit around the ladder's top and bottom miter cuts, respectively, and the timbers' arrises fit against the back wall's inside facing. The faces of the Gym's inside short timbers should meet the back wall's edge, and the open portion of its cube-like shape should face toward the front of the Tarzanium. If you have trouble keeping the Gym in correct alignment as you attach it, tack it temporarily to the Tarzanium's back wall with 16d casing nails toe-nailed part of the way in. Pull these nails out once the Gym is permanently installed and touch up the nail holes with spackling and paint.

17. The top and bottom timbers are attached to the back wall with three 1/4" x 6" hex-head bolts at each timber. The bolt holes (A) are counterbored, and because the two timbers are turned diagonally toward the wall's inside facing, the bore holes for these bolts are made from arris to arris (through the timber's diagonal) rather than through opposite faces. Checking the illustration for layouts, first bore three 1" x 3"-deep counterbores through the rounded arris of each timber.

18. Use your 1/4" extension bit to bore through-holes in the centers of the 1" counterbores, right through the timbers and on through the back wall. Make every effort to bore these holes straight so that they'll pierce the 1-1/2" x 3-1/2" pieces hidden inside the Tarzanium's wall; bores through the wall's plywood facings alone are insufficient to secure the Gym firmly in place.

19. Finally, carefully bore 1" x 1/2"-deep counterbores centered on the 1/4" through-holes in the wall's outside facing.

20. Insert a bolt with washer into each hole from the wall's outside. To secure the Gym tightly in place, tighten a nut with washer onto the threaded end of the bolt. Use your needle-nose locking pliers to secure the bolt's head while you tighten the nut with your ratchet wrench. Retighten the bolts from time to time to keep your Gym sturdy.

Cool Slide

This super slide features a cool and slippery laminate surface, which prevents the burns caused by metal slides. Ready, set, slide!

CUT LIST

2	1-1/2" x 7-1/4" x 103-1/2"	Rails
2	1-1/2" x 3-1/2" x 94"	Supports
7	1-1/2" x 3-1/2" x 18"	Blocking
2	3/4" x 1-1/2" x 94-7/8"	Trim
1	3/4" x 21" x 94" plywood	Substrate
1	20-3/4" x 94" white plastic laminate	Slide
1	3/4" x 4-5/16" x 21"	End cap
2	3-1/2" x 3-1/2" x 24"	Gate posts

HARDWARE AND SUPPLIES

5/16" x 2-1/2" lag screws with washers (6)
Laminate cement (1 quart)
2-1/2" deck screws (1 pound)
1-1/2" deck screws (5)
16d casing nails (2 pounds)
6d casing nails (1 pound)
4d casing nails (20)
Exterior alkyd primer
Alkyd enamel paint
Mineral spirits

SUGGESTED TOOLS

Layout tools
Claw hammer
Panel saw
Hacksaw
Flat file
Ratchet wrench with 1/2" socket and extension arm
Circular saw
Jigsaw
3/8" drill
5/16" brad-point bit
1-1/4" Forstner bit or self-feeding bit
Pilot bits to match screw sizes
Router
3/8" rounding-over bit
Belt sander
Orbital sander
Laminate roller
Paintbrushes
2" paintbrush for laminate cement

TIPS

- Use the dimensions in the Cut List as indicators of rough length only; rely on the instruction steps for exact shaping of mitered ends and other details.
- Purchase the laminate, laminate cement, and laminate roller from a dealer of cabinetmaking supplies. Unless you own a table saw and a triple-chip laminate-cutting saw blade, have the laminate cut there or at a cabinet shop.
- This project requires both the modification of one metal side rail on the Tarzanium project and the addition of two gate posts.
- For suggestions on providing a safe impact zone at the bottom end of the slide, see pages 29 and 31.

INSTRUCTIONS

1. Begin by cutting the two 1-1/2" x 7-1/4" rails to a rough length of 103-1/2".

2. Examine the Cool Slide illustrations on pages 57 and 58 to familiarize yourself with how the two rails support the laminated slide assembly between the ground and the Tarzanium's platform. The bottom edge nearest to the upper end of each rail has a notched, angled cutout that fits over the platform; above these notches, counterbored lag screws secure each rail to the inside face of a gate post. The lower end of each rail has a double miter cut where the slide rests on the ground. The slide is positioned at an angle of 30° from the horizontal.

3. To cut the upper corner of each rail, first set a rail face up in front of you so that its lower end is to the left and its upper end is to the right. With your protractor lined up with the edge farthest from you, lay out a 60° angled line that starts at the right-hand corner farthest from you and angles toward you across the face of the rail. Cut the line with your circular saw.

4. From the upper point of the cut, measure 4-3/4" down the cut and mark on the top face. Next, from that mark, square a 2-1/4" line along the face. Then, from the 2-1/4" point, square a line to the rail's bottom edge. See the Cool Slide illustration for a view of this cutout.

5. Use your circular saw and jigsaw to remove the cutout.

6. Round the sharp top and bottom corners of the rail by laying out a 3/4" radius at each one. Cut the radii with your jigsaw.

7. Lay out a 1-1/4" x 1/2"-deep counterbore in the rail's face, centered 1-1/8" from the 60° cut and 2" above the 2-1/4" edge. Drill the counterbore and then use a 5/16" bit to bore a through-hole in the counterbore's center.

8. Move to the rail's lower end. Using the squared end as your reference, lay out a 4"-long, 60° line on the rail's face to intersect the bottom edge of the rail. Then cut the line.

9. From the intersection of the cut and the original squared end of the rail, square a line to the top edge of the rail and then cut the squared line. The result should be a double miter, the saw cuts of which meet in a 90° angle.

10. With your router setup, round over all arrises except the 90° cutout at the rail's top end. Do round over the 3/4" radius located at the bottom corner of the cutout; this will help keep that corner from injuring children playing beneath the slide.

11. To lay out the second rail, either repeat the layouts in Steps 2 through 10 or use the cut rail as a template. Simply lay the cut rail on top of the second rail, align the edges and ends, and scribe the second rail from the first. Saw the second rail to shape and round over identical arrises. Take care, however, to drill the counterbore into the opposite face of the second rail.

12. Sand the rails thoroughly, wipe off the sanding debris, and prime and paint them. Allow them to dry thoroughly while you're building the laminated slide assembly.

13. The slide assembly consists of two supports with pieces of blocking between them and a plywood piece that's attached to the frame's top edges. Begin the assembly by laying out and cutting the seven pieces of blocking to 21" lengths.

14. Maintaining its total length at 94", lay out a support with a 60° angle across its face from the corner at one end. Cut the angled line and repeat to lay out and cut the second support.

15. The framework is assembled using a pair of 16d casing nails at each joint. Fasten the first piece of blocking between the supports so that its outermost face aligns with the lower (square) ends of the supports and its top and bottom edges align with those of the supports. Then fasten five more pieces of blocking between the supports, centering them at 16" intervals and aligning the edges as before.

16. To bevel-cut the final piece of blocking, set the circular-saw blade for a 30° cut. Then, using an arris as your guide, cut along the length of the blocking's face to create a beveled edge.

17. Mount this piece of blocking between the supports as shown in the illustration.

18. Turn the framework upside down, with the miter cuts facing up. Use your router setup to round over all arrises except for the two long outside arrises of the supports and the square and mitered ends.

19. Lay out the plywood substrate. Begin by laying out and ripping a 21"-wide x 94" piece of 3/4" plywood. Then make a bevel cut at one 21" edge of the plywood by setting the circular-saw blade at 30°; guide the saw along the plywood's face, using the arris of the edge as your guide.

20. Turn the slide assembly right side up so that the mitered ends face down. Using 6d casing nails, attach the plywood substrate to the top edges of the assembly; align the short point of its mitered end with the long points of the supports. Space the nails approximately 5" apart, nailing through the braces as well as along the supports; be sure to drive the nails' heads flush with the substrate's surface.

21. Ask a friend for help with this step. Begin by clearing a dust-free work area large enough for both the substrate and the laminate. Make sure the substrate's top surface is free of sawdust and turn the laminate so that its finished surface faces down. Coat the top surfaces of both the laminate and the substrate with a thin, even coating of laminate cement, following the directions on the can. Let the coats dry as indicated in the directions and recoat both surfaces lightly to ensure complete coverage.

22. When the cement has set up, space a half-dozen thin, dust-free pieces of scrap wood across the substrate's glued surface at regular intervals. (Glue-covered surfaces bond together instantly upon contact; the scrap wood will allow you to align the laminate in approximate position without actually gluing it to the substrate.) Carefully set the laminate onto the scrap pieces so that the laminate's ends align with the substrate's ends and the laminate is centered between the substrate's long edges. Now, gently remove the scrap piece closest to the substrate's beveled end, gluing the laminate and the plywood together so that they're exactly aligned at the tip of the bevel. Then remove the remaining scraps one by one, gluing as you go.

23. To ensure a permanent bond, use a laminate roller to apply even pressure across every part of the laminate, pressing hard as you move the roller about. Pay particular attention to the two narrow edges of the laminate, which, unlike the long edges, won't receive protective trim strips.

24. Position the rails on the slide assembly's sides, with their counterbores facing each other across the slide's upper end. Align the bottom edges of the rails and slide assembly and make sure the uppermost blocking piece's outside face is aligned with the 5" ends of the rails' cutouts. Fasten the rails to the assembly by driving groups of four 2-1/2" deck screws through each rail's inside face between each pair of blocking pieces; space the groups of screws in pairs 12" apart.

25. Using 3/4" x 5-1/2" stock, lay out and cut the end cap to 21" in length. Then lay out and rip the width to 4-5/16".

COOL SLIDE

3½" x 3½" x 24"
POST

1¼"

1¼" x ½"
COUNTERBORE
W/ 5/16" THROUGH
HOLE

20¾"

11½"

3/4" x 1½" x 94⅞"
TRIM

2¼"

1½" x 3½" x 18"
BEVELED
BLOCKING

LAMINATE

103½"

3/4" x 21" x 94"
PLYWOOD
SUBSTRATE

1½" x 3½" x 18"
BLOCKING

1½" x 7¼" x 103½"
SLIDE RAIL

16"

1½" x 3½" x 94"
SUPPORT

16"

3/4" x 4⁵/16" x 21"
END CAP

26. Set the end cap with its widest face up and use your router setup to round over a single arris on one 21" edge.

27. Sand the end cap, remove the sanding dust, and prime and paint the cap to match the rails.

28. The end cap fastens against the outside face of the blocking piece at the lower end of the slide; the radiused arris should be turned up and away from the laminate so that the square arris on the same edge aligns exactly with the top of the plastic laminate. Fasten the end cap to the blocking and support ends with 6d casing nails.

29. Lay out a 30° miter on each end of each 3/4" x 1-1/2" trim piece, using the 3/4" edges as your reference points. The miters on each piece are aligned alike, and the total length of each trim piece should be 94-7/8".

30. Set a trim piece face up and radius all arrises on the top face except for the edge closest to you. Repeat to rout the other trim piece in similar but opposite fashion. (Each piece of trim is applied to an inside face of a rail.)

31. Sand, prime, and paint the two trim pieces.

32. Position the trim pieces so that their square edges fit tightly against the slide's laminate surface and their square faces fasten against each rail's inside face. Align the short point of each trim piece's upper end with the top edge of the laminate. Drive 4d casing nails, spaced about 8" apart, through each trim piece's radiused face.

33. Cut the gate posts to 24" lengths. Set a post face up and, at one end, lay out a pair of 45° miters on opposite faces. Cut them with your circular saw set for 45° cutting; finish the cuts with your panel saw. Repeat with the other gate post.

34. Set a gate post with one flat face up. Then lay out a 3-7/8"-long x 2-1/4"-deep cutout at its square end. (The cutout should be on the inside face of the post.) After squaring the layouts around adjacent faces, make the cutout with your circular saw and panel saw. Repeat to make an identical cutout in the second post.

35. Mark one post for the 1-1/4" side-railing holes. Turn the post so that the cutout's inside face is vertical and facing toward your right. Locate both holes on the top face, 1-1/4" from the post's inside (or right-hand) face. The lowest hole (the one nearest the cutout) should be 11-1/2" above the cutout's 2-1/4" face and should be 1" deep. The upper hole is a through-hole and is located 20-3/4" above the same 2-1/4" face.

36. Bore the second post in a similar manner to the first but make the 1"-deep hole on the opposite face. (Each 1"-deep hole accepts an end of a shortened side rail, as shown in the Placement Detail.)

37. In the bottom outside face of each post, make two 1-1/4" x 1/2"-deep counterbores. Center one hole 1" from an edge and 1" from the bottom end of the post; center the other hole 1" from the opposite edge and 2-3/4" from the bottom. Then bore a 5/16" through-hole in each counterbore's center. (The through-holes should exit from the cutout's face.)

38. Use your router setup to round over all arrises on the posts except for those of the cutouts.

39. Sand the posts, wipe away the sanding dust, and prime and paint the posts as desired.

40. If you've already installed the side railings on the Tarzanium, loosen the bolts and lag screws on one wall and remove one pair of railings.

41. With your hacksaw, cut an 8" and a 36" section from one piece of railing; ease the cut edges with your file.

42. Position the posts by placing their cutouts over the platform's edge. Facing the platform with the back wall to your right, position the right-hand post so that its right-hand face is 6-1/2" from the back wall's inside facing. Locate the second post so that a 24" distance separates the two posts' inside faces. Insert the side rails as you locate the posts. Then, for each lag screw, bore a 1/4"-diameter pilot hole through each counterbore in the posts. Use two 5/16" x 2-1/2" lag screws with washers to fasten each post in place.

43. With a hand from your helper, set the slide into place between the posts, aligning the two cutouts tightly against the platform's edge. Bore 1/4" pilot holes through the counterbores and into the posts, use your ratchet wrench to fasten the lag screws with washers—and relax!

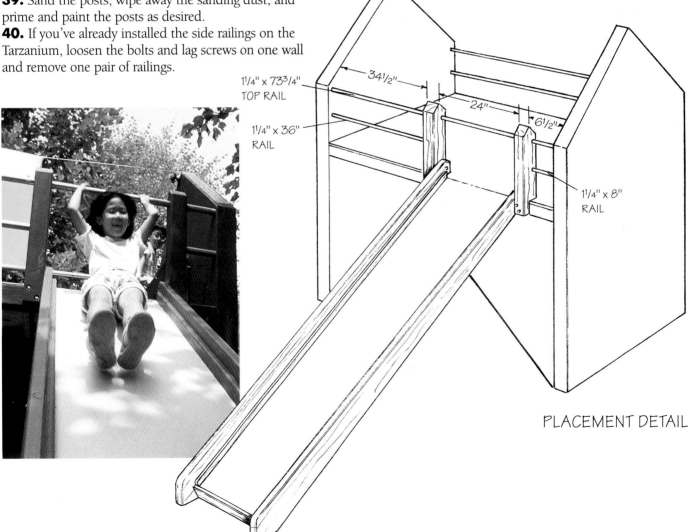

1¹/₄" x 73³/₄" TOP RAIL

1¹/₄" x 36" RAIL

34¹/₂"

24"

6¹/₂"

1¹/₄" x 8" RAIL

PLACEMENT DETAIL

Mountain Rope

This exciting alpine-style climbing rope is just the kind of challenge kids love.

CUT LIST

6 1-1/2" x 3-1/2" x 3-1/2"   Blocks

HARDWARE AND SUPPLIES

3" deck screws (12)
12' of 3/4" sisal rope
Plastic tape
Exterior alkyd primer
Alkyd enamel paint
Mineral spirits

SUGGESTED TOOLS

Layout tools
No. 2 screwdriver
Circular saw
3/8" drill
1" brad-point bit
Pilot bit to match screw size
Router
3/8" rounding-over bit
Orbital sander
1" paintbrush

TIPS

- If a pilot bit for 3" screws is unavailable, first use a 3/32" twist-drill bit to bore for the screws' shafts and then use a countersink bit to bore for the screws' heads.
- Allow plenty of 1-1/2" x 3-1/2" stock to safely cut the blocks to size.
- If the Tarzanium is located far from a power source, use a brace and 1" bit to bore the hole for the rope (see Step 8).

INSTRUCTIONS

1. Lay out the six blocks and cut them to shape with your circular saw.

2. Bore two pilot holes for 3" deck screws through the face of each block, placing the holes diagonally across from each other and 1" from their respective corners.

3. Secure a block face up in a vise or otherwise secure it. Then, with your router setup, round all the arrises on the top face. Repeat with the other five blocks.

4. Sand the blocks thoroughly and wipe away the sanding debris.

5. Prime and paint the blocks.

6. Use your measuring tape and framing square (and the illustration as a guide) to lay out the locations of the blocks on the outside plywood facing of the Tarzanium's back wall. Each block is mounted diagonally, with its square face against the plywood, and each vertical row of three blocks is centered 16-1/2" from a long edge of the plywood facing. The lowest block is centered 12" above the wall's bottom; the second block is centered at 21-1/2". The remaining blocks center above the first two at 19" intervals.

7. Mount the blocks with 3" deck screws as shown. The screws are driven through the plywood facing along a vertical line so that they'll enter the two center studs inside of the front wall. (Blocks mounted on the 1/2" plywood facing alone are not sufficient to support a child's weight.)

8. Complete the remaining steps while standing on the Tarzanium's platform. Lay out a 1" bore hole for the rope, 1-3/4" down from the peak of the front wall. Then bore right through the wall, carefully avoiding any nails. (Shift the location of the bore hole slightly if nails are in the way.)

9. Sand the rough edges of both sides of the bore hole.

10. Slip one end of the 3/4" rope through the hole from the outside and double-knot the rope on the inside of the wall. Then knot the rope every 10" or so and cut its length to suit. To prevent the rope from unraveling, wrap its two ends tightly with plastic tape.

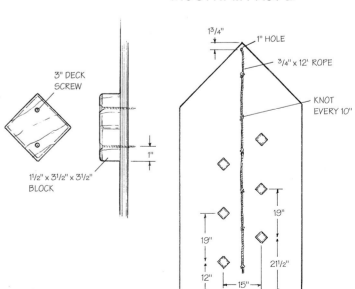

MOUNTAIN ROPE

3" DECK SCREW

1½" x 3½" x 3½" BLOCK

1"

1¾"

1" HOLE

¾" x 12' ROPE

KNOT EVERY 10"

19"

19"

21½"

12"

15"

The all-time favorite for fantasy play, this easy project is designed to tuck into a quiet corner of the Tarzanium.

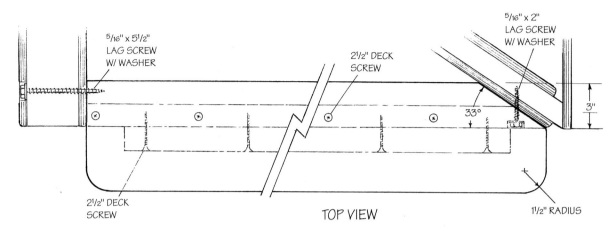

TOP VIEW

CUT LIST

1	1-1/2" x 7-1/4" x 70-3/4"	Seat
1	1-1/2" x 5-1/2" x 72"	Seat support
1	1-1/2" x 1-1/2" x 66"	Brace

HARDWARE AND SUPPLIES

5/16" x 5-1/2" lag screws (2)
5/16" x 2" lag screws (2)
5/16" cut washers (4)
2-1/2" deck screws (21)
5' x 7' 6-mil polyethylene plastic sheeting
1/4" staples
Exterior alkyd primer
Alkyd enamel paint
Mineral spirits
Play sand (25 pounds); see "Tips"

SUGGESTED TOOLS

Layout tools
Claw hammer
Ratchet wrench with 1/2" socket
Craft knife (or utility knife)
Staple gun
Circular saw
Panel saw
Jigsaw
3/8" drill
1-1/4" Forstner bit (or 1-1/4" self-feeding bit)
5/16" brad-point bit
Pilot bit to match screw size

Router
3/8" rounding-over bit
Belt sander
Orbital sander
Paintbrushes
Compass
Adjustable protractor (see "Tips")

TIPS

- Packaged play sand is available at many building-supply centers. If you can't find this product, choose the cleanest fine-grained sand available.
- If you don't own an adjustable protractor, use a standard protractor and a straightedge instead.

INSTRUCTIONS

1. Lay out and cut the seat to 70-3/4" in length. Then, with the seat facing up and stretched horizontally in front of you, measure 3" down from the edge that is farthest from you and mark the end. Square through the mark on the end; also mark the top face at that point.

2. Hold an adjustable protractor set for 33° against the marked end so that the protractor's beam (or arm) aligns with the mark on the face; strike a pencil line (along the beam) on the face. The line should intersect the seat edge that is farthest from you to create a right triangle, the hypotenuse (longest edge) of which is 5-3/8" long. (The 33° setting matches the 33° angle of the window wall.)

3. Cut the line with your circular saw.

4. On the top face, lay out a 1-1/2" radius at each corner of the uncut 70-3/4" edge. Cut these two radii with your jigsaw.

5. With the seat support face up, square a line across one face, exactly 70-3/4" from an end. Then set your adjustable protractor for 33° and use it to mark a bevel from the squared line across an edge so that the bevel "returns" toward the main part of the support. Square across the opposite face, using the short point of the bevel as your starting point.

6. Secure the support so that the edge with the bevel mark faces up and start a cut through the mark with your panel saw. Cut carefully through the support, using the squared lines on the faces as guides.

7. Lay out two 1-1/4" counterbored holes on the support's top face, spaced 4" apart and located 2" from the beveled end. Bore both holes 1/2" deep and then use a 5/16" drill bit to bore through the center of each counterbore, piercing the bevel cut on the other side.

8. Lay out and cut the 66" brace to length.

9. Center the brace on the unbeveled face of the seat support, aligning it with the support's top edge. Fasten the brace with 2-1/2" deck screws spaced approximately 7" apart.

10. Position the seat on top of the seat support and brace; the seat's inside edge should be 1-1/2" from the inside face of the seat support, and the long point of the

END VIEW

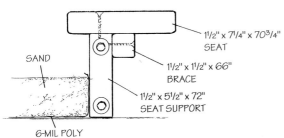

SAND

1¹/₂" x 7¹/₄" x 70³/₄"
SEAT

1¹/₂" x 1¹/₂" x 66"
BRACE

1¹/₂" x 5¹/₂" x 72"
SEAT SUPPORT

6-MIL POLY

seat support's bevel should be aligned with the long point of the seat's mitered end. Fasten the seat to the seat support's edge, using pilot-bored 2-1/2" deck screws spaced approximately 7" apart and driven through the seat's top face.

11. With your router setup, round all arrises of the seat except those on the square and mitered ends.

12. Sand the seat assembly, using your belt and orbital sanders when possible and sanding by hand when neces-

sary. Remove the sanding debris with a tack rag.

13. Prime the sandbox and then apply two coats of paint.

14. To fasten the square end of the seat support to the front wall of the Tarzanium, first make two 1-1/4" counterbores, each 1/2"-deep, in the front wall's outside facing. Space the holes 4" apart and center them 3/4" from the edge of the outside facing that is nearest the door opening. Center the lower counterbore 1" above the wall's bottom edge.

15. Use a drill and 5/16" brad-point bit to bore from the outside facing through the centers of the two counterbores.

16. Position the seat assembly between the front and back walls. Then use a claw hammer to drive two 5-1/2" lag screws through the front wall's bore holes into the end of the seat assembly. Tighten the screws with a ratchet wrench, checking to be sure the end of the wall and the front face of the support are aligned.

17. Start two 2" lag screws through the counterbores in the face of the support and into the window wall. Tighten these lag screws as before.

18. To keep the sand separated from the turf below, use your craft or utility knife to cut a doubled layer of 6-mil polyethylene plastic sheeting to size; fit the plastic into the sandbox so that a 3"-high lip of plastic surrounds the triangular shape. Then, using your staple gun and staples, fasten the edges of the plastic to the seat support.

19. Fill the sandbox with 3" of sand. Keeping the sand clean and providing a few digging tools will encourage regular play!

Sunshade

Hot days can be cooled considerably by adding this colorful tarp to your kid's Tarzanium. Youngsters will also love the tent-like sense of privacy it provides.

CUT LIST
None

HARDWARE AND SUPPLIES
32" x 62" ripstop nylon
1/4" grommets (8)
10' of 1/4" nylon rope
Screw eyes; wire size 7 (2)

SUGGESTED TOOLS
Layout tools
3/8" drill
1/8" twist-drill bit
Claw hammer
Slip-joint pliers
Craft knife
Scissors
Grommet setter with anvil
Kitchen matches

TIPS
■ Purchase the ripstop nylon at a fabric store. If the store doesn't stock this fabric, hem a slightly larger piece of ordinary nylon to the dimensions given in the Hardware and Supplies list.
■ The grommets, grommet setter, and anvil can be purchased at a crafts store.

INSTRUCTIONS

1. Cut the fabric to size. Also cut seven 10" lengths of 1/4" nylon rope to make the short ties; the remaining 50" piece will serve as the long tie. To prevent the ties' ends from unraveling, carefully melt them with a lit kitchen match. (Caution: Dripping liquified nylon can cause serious burns.)

2. Lay out eight marks on the flat fabric: one at each corner, exactly 1" from each edge; and one 1" from each edge, exactly halfway along each side.

3. Place a piece of wood scrap underneath one of the marks on the fabric. Use your craft knife to cut a hole approximately 5/16" in diameter at the mark. Repeat to cut holes at every mark around the fabric's perimeter.

4. Use the grommet setter to set a grommet at each hole.

5. Knot one end of the long tie to a grommet hole in one long side of the fabric. Then knot a short tie to each of the remaining grommeted holes; these knots should be in the ties' middles, leaving two equal lengths of rope at each short-tie location.

6. To bore holes for the screw eyes on each of the Tarzanium's two walls, use your 1/8" twist-drill bit. Bore a hole 1" below the peak of each inside facing. Use your slip-joint pliers to secure the screw eyes to the wood.

7. The free end of the long tie mounts to the back wall's screw eye, and the short tie opposite to it mounts to the screw eye in the wall. Mount the short tie first. The remaining ties wrap around the Tarzanium's metal side rails to secure the shade in "tent-fashion."

8. Tugging on the Sun Shade will quickly ruin it, so let your kids know that this project is not for use as a plaything. Because weather changes will cause the shade's ties to stretch, you'll need to tighten them occasionally to restore the shade's shape.

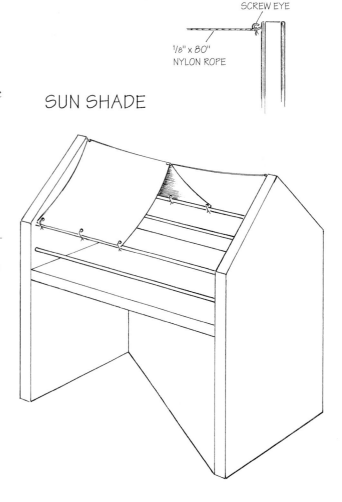

SCREW EYE

1/8" x 80" NYLON ROPE

SUN SHADE

BIG STABLE

The grand scale and weather-resistant materials of this project make it a young horse-lover's dream, and what better location for a stable than under the open sky?

CUT LIST

1	5/8" x 12" x 20" plywood	Base
1	5/8" x 12" x 14-7/8" plywood	Back wall
1	5/8" x 12" x 14-7/8" plywood	Front wall
2	5/8" x 9" x 17-1/2" plywood	Roof panels
1	5/8" x 3-1/4" x 9" plywood	Overhang
1	1-1/2" x 2" x 5"	Cap
1	1/4" x 6" dowel	Flagpole
1	1/2" x 5/8" x 20"	Bottom rail
2	1/2" x 5/8" x 16-5/8"	Outside rails
2	1/2" x 5/8" x 3-3/4"	Short posts
1	1/2" x 5/8" x 10-3/4"	Outside long post
2	1/2" x 5/8" x 6-1/8"	Inside long rails
1	1/2" x 5/8" x 5-5/8"	Inside short rail
3	1/2" x 5/8" x 14-7/8"	Inside long posts
30	1/2" x 5/8" x 7"	Long fence rails
6	1/2" x 5/8" x 1-1/2"	Short fence rails
11	1/8" 3-3/4" dowel	Connectors
2	1/4" x 3/4" x 17-1/2"	Roof edgings

HARDWARE AND SUPPLIES

1" x 5" ripstop nylon flag
1-1/2" deck screws (19)
2-1/2" deck screws (2)
No. 18 x 3/4" brads (1 box)
Resin glue
Water sealer

SUGGESTED TOOLS

Layout tools
Claw hammer
Coping saw
Backsaw
Circular saw
Jigsaw
3/8" drill
1/8" brad-point bit
1/4" brad-point bit
Pilot bits to match screw sizes
Orbital sander
Scissors

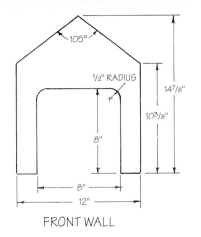

FRONT WALL

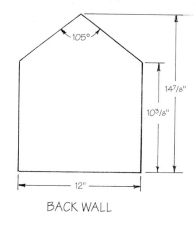

BACK WALL

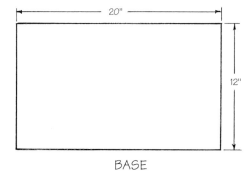

BASE

TIPS

■ This project is scaled for play horses with maximum heights of 9". If your child's animals are larger or smaller, scale the project dimensions as necessary.

■ The 1/4" x 3/4" stock is a type of trim known as *screen mold*; it's available at building-supply centers.

■ The 1/2" x 5/8" stock is a type of wood trim known as *parting bead*. If it's unavailable in your area, substitute a similar trim (and adjust the Cut List's dimensions accordingly) or rip your own trim to 1/2" x 5/8".

■ On a project with many small parts, sand the parts as the assembly progresses rather than sanding the finished assembly all at once.

INSTRUCTIONS

1. Using the illustrations as guides, lay out the base and wall pieces on 5/8" plywood. Note that the roof edges are each 7-1/2" long. Cut the three pieces to size with your table saw.

2. Set the front wall face up and lay out the centered 8" x 8" doorway on it; also lay out a 1/2" radius at each of the doorway's top corners. Cut out the marked doorway with your circular saw and jigsaw.

3. Each roof panel (see page 69) is bevel cut along both 17-1/2" edges. The two bevels on each panel are aligned the same way, and the distance between the long point and the short point of the bevels is 8-1/2" across the face. After laying the panels out, cut them to 17-1/2" in length. Then set your circular-saw blade for a 37° bevel cut and bevel the four edges of the two panels.

4. Place the 12" edge of the back wall on the face of the base, adjacent to one 12" edge. Fasten the pieces together with three equally spaced, pilot-bored 1-1/2" deck screws driven through the bottom of the base and into the edge of the wall.

5. Position the front wall parallel to the back wall so that the inside faces of each wall are 15-3/8" apart. Fasten the front wall with one 1-1/2" screw driven into each 2" bottom edge.

6. Secure each roof panel in place by driving six equally spaced 1-1/2" screws through each panel and into the top edges of the walls, 3/4" from each short edge. Two beveled edges of the two panels should meet at the roof's peak, and the panels should overhang the outside faces of the walls by 3/8".

7. Lay out the 9"-long overhang on 5/8" plywood; its bevel angle is 45°. The distance between one bevel's short point and the other's long point is 2-3/4". Cut the piece with your circular saw.

8. Center the overhang above the doorway, locating the short point of one bevel 1-1/4" above the top edge of the cutout. Use resin glue and a few No. 18 x 3/4" brads to attach the overhang in place.

9. Rip the 2"-wide cap from a scrap of 1-1/2" x 3-1/2" stock that's at least 24" long.

10. Set the stock on a 1-1/2" edge and secure it by fastening a clamp near one end. Set your circular-saw blade at 37° and for a 1" depth of cut. Then, using the long arris of the top face as your guide line, make a bevel cut along the top face into the stock. Turn and reclamp the stock to make an identical bevel cut, this time using the top face's other arris as your guide line. (This cut should free a triangularly sectioned piece of waste.) Finally, with your circular-saw blade reset at 90°, cut the cap piece to 5" in length.

11. Sand the cap and fasten it to the roof peak by driving two pilot-bored 2-1/2" deck screws through the top face of the cap and into the roof panels; locate the screws diagonally from each other so that each one is centered 1/2" from an end and 1/2" from a 5" edge.

12. Using your backsaw and a miter box to cut the posts and rails will guarantee square cuts. First, lay out and cut three inside long posts to 14-7/8" in length; on each one, cut one end square and the other end with a 37° miter cut, using the 5/8" face as your reference. (The length refers to the longest dimension, from the square end to the long point of the miter.)

13. Lay out and cut the outside long post. Its length is 10-3/4", measured from a square end to the long point of a 37° miter cut.

14. Referring to the Cut List, lay out and cut to length the two inside long rails, the inside short rail, the two short posts, the two outside rails, and the bottom rail. Each has square ends.

15. A delicate touch is required here! The posts and rails are fastened to the Big Stable's plywood parts or to each other with brads. Before driving the brads, square and mark the joints with your measuring tape and try square. First, fasten the two outside rails and the bottom rail to the plywood exterior as shown in the Rail Detail. Next, fasten groups of parts together as "mini-assemblies" consisting of one inside post, one outside post, and an inside rail. Then install each three-piece unit within the stable.

16. Cut the two pieces of roof edging to length and fasten them to the roof's outermost edges with brads, aligning the edges and ends as you do.

17. Bore a 1/4" hole, 3/4" deep, into the center of the cap's top face. Cut the 1/4" dowel flagpole to 6" in length and glue it into the bore hole.

18. Use your coping saw to create a 1"-deep slot down through the center of the flagpole's end. Then cut the ripstop nylon flag so that it has a 1"-wide end. Fasten the flag in the slot with a bit of glue.

19. The fence consists of ten sections that fasten together by means of 1/8" dowel connectors. These connectors, which are glued only at the ends, allow the sections to rotate freely to create whatever fence shape your kids might want. Examine the Fence Detail noting that the 1/8" bore holes for the connectors are centered 1/4" from the fence rails' ends and are bored through the 1/2" faces of the long and short fence rails.

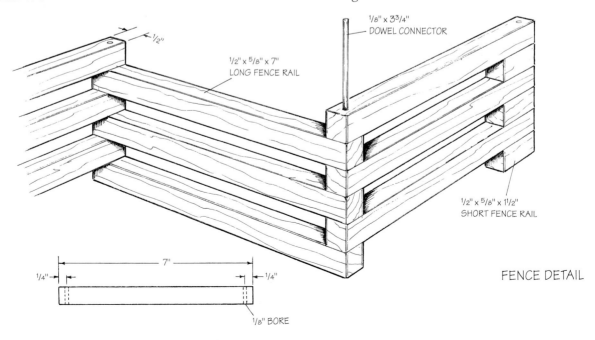

1/8" x 3 3/4"
DOWEL CONNECTOR

1/2" x 5/8" x 7"
LONG FENCE RAIL

1/2" x 5/8" x 1 1/2"
SHORT FENCE RAIL

1/2"

7"

1/4"

1/4"

1/8" BORE

FENCE DETAIL

20. Begin by cutting the long and short fence rails and the dowel connectors to length. Use your drill and 1/8" bit to bore the holes straight through their faces. Then sand the rails well and wipe away the dust when you're through.

21. Assemble an end section first, using three long rails, three short rails, and a connector. The short rails' faces are glued to the long rails so that the ends of all the rails are flush. Set the stack of rails so that a short rail is on the bottom and place a drop of glue into the bottom hole. Then drive a connector down through the top hole.

22. The next section's ends fasten to the free ends of the first. Keep adding sections, alternating the arrangement of the rails so that the fence will sit flat when completed; glue the connectors into the bottom rails only. Finish the fence with an end section that is identical to the first end section but that's upside down. As the glue is drying, manipulate the sections freely from time to time to ensure that no section's connector joint dries stiffly due to misplaced glue.

23. Sand away any bits of dried glue, wipe the dust away, and finish your Big Stable with two coats of water sealer.

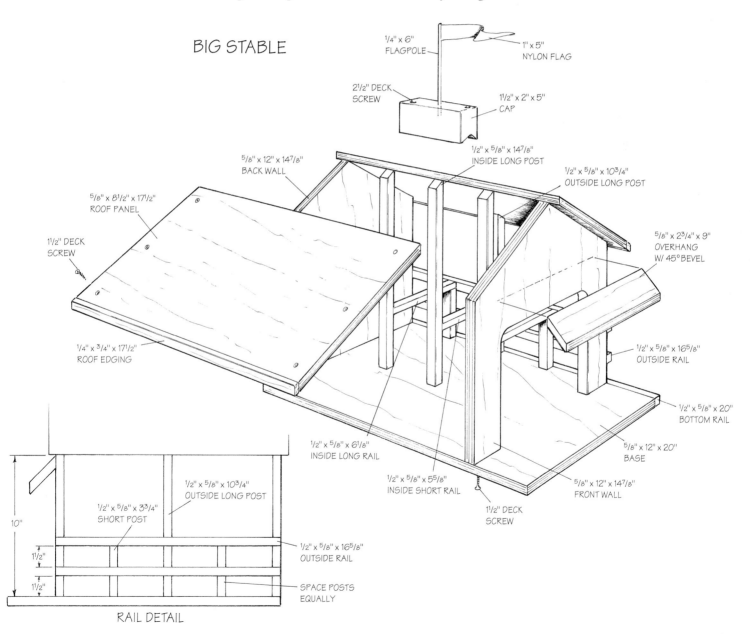

BIG STABLE

1/4" x 6" FLAGPOLE

1" x 5" NYLON FLAG

2½" DECK SCREW

1½" x 2" x 5" CAP

5/8" x 12" x 14⁷/₈" BACK WALL

1/2" x 5/8" x 14⁷/₈" INSIDE LONG POST

1/2" x 5/8" x 10³/₄" OUTSIDE LONG POST

5/8" x 8½" x 17½" ROOF PANEL

5/8" x 2³/₄" x 9" OVERHANG W/ 45° BEVEL

1½" DECK SCREW

1/2" x 5/8" x 16⁵/₈" OUTSIDE RAIL

1/4" x ³/₄" x 17½" ROOF EDGING

1/2" x 5/8" x 20" BOTTOM RAIL

5/8" x 12" x 20" BASE

1/2" x 5/8" x 6¹/₈" INSIDE LONG RAIL

1/2" x 5/8" x 5⁵/₈" INSIDE SHORT RAIL

1½" DECK SCREW

5/8" x 12" x 14⁷/₈" FRONT WALL

1/2" x 5/8" x 10³/₄" OUTSIDE LONG POST

1/2" x 5/8" x 3³/₄" SHORT POST

1/2" x 5/8" x 16⁵/₈" OUTSIDE RAIL

SPACE POSTS EQUALLY

10"

1½"

1½"

RAIL DETAIL

Fluid materials such as sand and water are unequaled for inviting imaginative play. This covered table holds them up where kids of all abilities can reach them, and its folding cover helps keep the elements (and unwelcome visitors such as cats and spiders) outside.

CUT LIST

1	3/4" x 24" x 40" plywood	Bottom
2	3/4" x 12-5/8" x 41-1/2" plywood	Lids
2	3/4" x 3-1/2" x 24" plywood	Short sides
2	3/4" x 3-1/2" x 41-1/2" plywood	Long sides
4	1-1/2" x 3-1/2" x 22"	Legs
2	1-1/2" x 3-1/2" x 18-1/2"	Leg braces
1	1-1/2" x 3-1/2" x 41-1/2"	Stretcher
1	1/4" x 1-1/2" x 41-1/2"	Lattice

HARDWARE AND SUPPLIES

1-1/4" deck screws (26)
1-3/4" deck screws (16)
2-1/2" deck screws (12)

Full-overlay pivot hinges (4)
3/4" brads (12)
Clear silicone caulk (1 tube)
Flush-fitting 1-1/4" (O.D.) drain kit with drain plug and at least 6" of drain line

SUGGESTED TOOLS

Layout tools
Claw hammer
Backsaw
Nos. 1 and 2 screwdrivers
Caulking gun
Circular saw
3/8" drill
3/8" brad-point bit
1-1/4" Forstner bit
3/16" extension bit
Pilot bits to match screw sizes
No. 2 drive bit
Router
3/8" rounding-over bit
Orbital sander

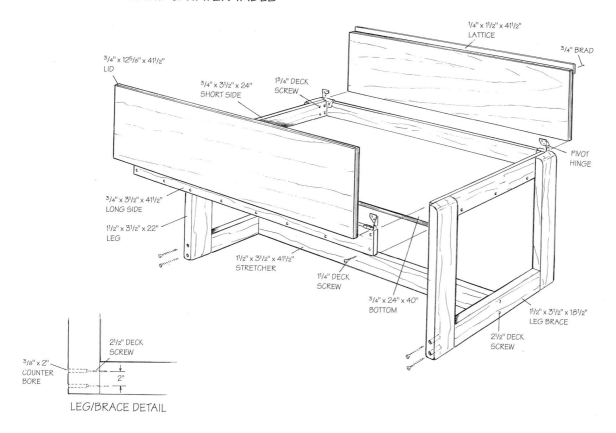

¹/₄" x 1¹/₂" x 41¹/₂"
LATTICE

³/₄" BRAD

³/₄" x 12⁵/₈" x 41¹/₂"
LID

³/₄" x 3¹/₂" x 24"
SHORT SIDE

1³/₄" DECK
SCREW

PIVOT
HINGE

³/₄" x 3¹/₂" x 41¹/₂"
LONG SIDE

1¹/₂" x 3¹/₂" x 22"
LEG

1¹/₂" x 3¹/₂" x 41¹/₂"
STRETCHER

1¹/₄" DECK
SCREW

³/₄" x 24" x 40"
BOTTOM

1¹/₂" x 3¹/₂" x 18¹/₂"
LEG BRACE

2¹/₂" DECK
SCREW

2¹/₂" DECK
SCREW

³/₈" x 2"
COUNTER
BORE

2"

LEG/BRACE DETAIL

TIPS

- Seek advice from your hardware or tool dealer when you're looking for the drain and the extension bit.
- To create pilot holes for the smaller hinge screws, use a sharp awl.

INSTRUCTIONS

1. Lay out the pieces. Then use your circular saw to cut them all except for the lattice, which should be cut with a backsaw. Label the parts before setting them aside.

2. Through the face of a long-side piece, bore a pair of pilot holes for 1-1/4" screws; locate these holes 3/8" from one end and 2-3/4" apart. Then bore identical holes near the other end of the side piece and both ends of the other long-side piece.

3. Bore six more identical pilot holes along the same face of each long-side piece, 3/8" from one long edge. Place the first hole 6" from an end and the others at 6" intervals.

4. Bore three identical holes along the face of each short-side piece, spacing the holes as in Step 3.

5. To assemble the box, first run a 3/16" bead of silicone caulk along the ends and edges of the bottom piece. Fasten the short-side pieces to the ends of the bottom piece, inserting 1-1/4" deck screws though the pilot-bored holes.

6. Apply caulk to the ends of the short-side pieces and fasten the two long sides to the edges of the bottom piece. Complete the box assembly by driving pairs of 1-1/4" screws at the corners; be sure to align the ends of the side pieces carefully.

7. To assemble the leg structure, first use your 3/8" brad-point bit to bore two 2"-deep counterbores into an edge of a leg. Center these holes along the leg's edge, locating them 3/4" and 2-3/4" from one end of the leg. Repeat to bore pairs of identical holes in the other three legs.

8. Chuck the 3/16" extension bit into your drill and set the bit's tip in the center of one counterbore. (The brad-point bit used in Step 7 creates a small impression that will guide the tip to the hole's center.) Bore through the leg's width. Repeat this step to bore 3/16" holes in the remaining legs' counterbores.

9. Set a leg brace on edge on your work surface. Butt the edge of a leg against it as shown in the Leg/Brace Detail, making sure the counterbores face outward. Next, use your No. 2 screwdriver to fasten two 2-1/2" screws through the counterbores and into the leg brace. Repeat to fasten another leg to the other end of the brace. Then assemble and fasten the second leg assembly.

10. Place a leg assembly flat down on some scrap wood and mark across the center of the brace at 9-1/4". Bore two pilot holes for 2-1/2" screws on this line, placing each hole 3/4" from an edge of the leg brace. Repeat to bore identical pilot holes in the other leg assembly.

11. Set the stretcher on edge and place a leg assembly against one end so that the holes in the brace are aligned with one end of the stretcher. Using a framing square to keep the stretcher and leg assembly at right angles to one another, fasten the assembly to the stretcher with two 2-1/2" screws inserted through the pilot holes. Repeat to fasten the other leg assembly to the other end of the stretcher. Set the assembly aside.

12. Through each inside corner of both short-side pieces, bore four pilot holes for 1-3/4" screws, spacing the holes to form a 2" x 2" square pattern and positioning the pattern as close as possible to the long-side pieces.

13. You'll probably need a hand with this step! Rest the assembled legs and stretcher on the ground and support the box assembly so that its corners are aligned with the tops of the legs (see the illustration). The top surfaces of the legs and sides should be flush. Fasten the legs in place with sixteen 1-3/4" screws inserted through the pilot-bored holes in the side pieces.

14. To assemble the two covers, first use your No. 1 screwdriver to fasten the hinges to each of the four corners of the box. Then align the lid pieces and fasten the hinges to them.

15. Position the lattice piece so that it covers the crack between the two lids. Using 3/4" brads, fasten it to one lid.

16. Using a router and 3/8" rounding-over bit, round any arrises you think might present a splinter hazard to your kids. Sand the table well and wipe away all the sanding debris.

17. To discourage water leakage, run a bead of silicone caulk around all the interior joints of the box; let the caulk dry. Then use the 1-1/4" Forstner bit to bore a hole in the bottom of the box. Install the drain kit in the hole and apply silicone caulk generously where the drain meets the plywood bottom.

18. Clean up any bits of debris before you load your table with play materials. *Play sand*—a clean, finely sifted product available at many building-supply centers—is superior to common sand. For water play, just provide a bucket or two and set your garden hose for a fine dribble.

FRESH MARKET

This magical market will thrill your young shoppers and encourage long hours of fantasy fun. It also doubles as a puppet theater, fort, or lemonade stand, and, when the play's over, it folds flat and stows away quickly and neatly. In the pages that follow, you'll find instructions for optional related projects: blackboards to fasten to its panels, a market basket, a grocery set, and a matching set of table and chairs.

CUT LIST

2	1/2" x 30" x 48" plywood	Front panels
2	1/2" x 28-1/2" x 28-1/2" x 30" plywood	Roof panels (see "Tips")
1	3/4" x 14-1/2" x 28" plywood	Countertop (see "Tips")
2	3/4" x 1-1/4" x 28-3/4"	Front top rails
2	3/4" x 1-1/4" x 28-3/4"	Front bottom rails
2	3/4" x 1-1/4" x 20-1/2"	Side window top rails
2	3/4" x 1-1/4" x 9-1/2"	Side window bottom rails
2	3/4" x 1-1/4" x 17-1/4"	Side window outside stiles
2	3/4" x 1-1/4" x 20-1/2"	Side window inside stiles
2	3/4" x 1-1/4" x 12-1/4"	Center window bottom rails
2	3/4" x 1-1/4" x 21-3/4"	Center window side stiles
2	3/4" x 1-1/4" x 30"	Roof bottom rails
4	3/4" x 1-1/4" x 27"	Roof side stiles
2	1-1/2" x 1-1/2" x 24"	Roof stops
2	1-1/4" x 65" dowel	Side poles
1	1-1/4" x 24-3/4" dowel	Bottom center pole
1	1-1/4" x 31" dowel	Top center pole

HARDWARE AND SUPPLIES

1" deck screws (1 pound)
1-1/4" deck screws (28)
2" deck screws (4)
2-1/2" deck screws (4)
30" of Jack chain
1-1/2" x 1-1/2" butt hinges with screws (9)
3" mending plate with screws
5" x 15" nylon fabric (3)
No. 18 x 1" brads (9)
Exterior alkyd primer
Alkyd enamel paint
Mineral spirits
Water sealer

SUGGESTED TOOLS

Layout tools
Claw hammer
Nos. 1 and 2 screwdrivers
Slip-joint pliers
Panel saw
Circular saw
Jigsaw
Half-round rasp (or spokeshave)
Router
3/8" rounding-over bit
3/8" drill
3/8" brad-point bit
Pilot bits to match screw sizes
No. 2 drive bit
Belt sander
Orbital sander
Sharp scissors
Paintbrushes

TIPS

■ Many of the 3/4" x 1-1/4" trim pieces listed in the Cut List have miter cuts on one or both ends. Use the Cut List only as a guide to each piece's total rough length; refer to Step 6 below and to the illustrations for details on scribing and cutting the trim pieces to their exact shape.

■ Before cutting the roof panels to size, see Step 5, and before cutting the countertop, see Step 19 and the Countertop illustration.

■ If you live in an especially windy location, you might want to stake down or otherwise brace your Fresh Market.

INSTRUCTIONS

1. Begin by sawing the two plywood front panels to size. Then secure one front panel with its best face down and lay out the window openings to the dimensions pictured in the Front Panel illustration. Note that one window is an irregular shape and the other is a two-sided cutout that opens onto one long edge of the plywood.

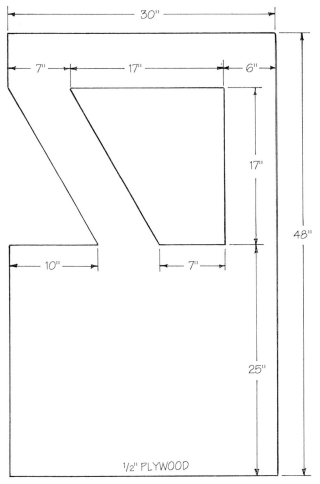

FRONT PANEL

2. With your circular saw, make a pocket cut (see page 19) into one side of the four-sided window opening, cutting as much of the line as possible. Repeat with the other three lines and then finish the cuts with a panel saw or jigsaw.

3. Saw the two-sided cutout, finishing the circular-saw cuts in the same manner as in Step 2.

4. Repeat Steps 1 through 3 to make a second front panel; its window shapes should be mirror images of those on the first front panel.

5. The two roof panels are isosceles triangles; each one has two equal angles and two sides of equal length. Lay out each triangle on 1/2" plywood stock, as shown in the Roof Panel illustration, and cut the panels to size with your circular saw.

6. Lay out and rip the 3/4" trim stock to 1-1/4" in width. Set a front panel with its best face up. Using the Fresh Market illustration as a guide, align the trim stock with the various plywood edges of the front panel, transferring the cutting lengths and angles onto your trim stock. Repeat to scribe the trim parts for the second front panel. Then cut all the trim pieces to size.

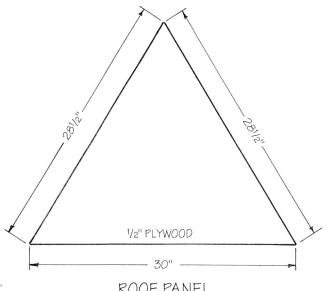

ROOF PANEL

FRESH MARKET

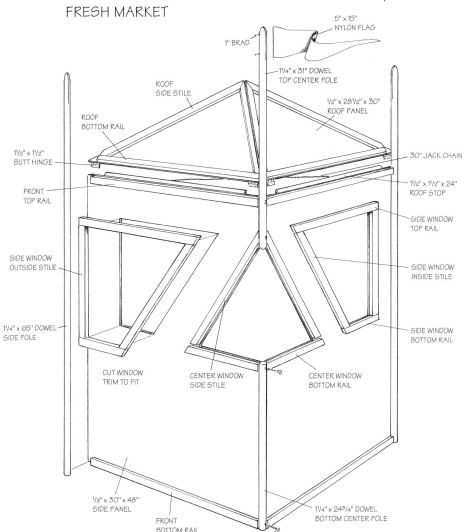

7. Attach the trim pieces to the plywood faces of the front panels by driving 1" deck screws, spaced 6" apart, from the inside (worst) face of the plywood. The easiest way to do this is to lean a front panel against a wall with its inside face toward you. Secure a trim piece to the plywood in its proper location and drive screws through the plywood's inside face.

8. Repeat Steps 6 and 7 to cut and attach trim pieces to the faces of the two roof panels. Because the roof panels are much smaller than the front panels, this work can be done on your work surface.

9. To fasten the butt hinges in place, first set the two front panels, trim side down and side by side, on a large flat surface such as a floor. The edges with the two-sided window openings should now form a single, triangular window opening. Set the two roof panels, trim side down, so that the longest edge of each aligns with the top edge of a front panel. (The top edge is the 30" edge nearest to the window openings.)

10. Place a hinge at each end of the 6"-long plywood joint above the center window and secure the hinges in place with the screws provided. Space three more hinges equally along the plywood joint below the same window, placing the two outermost at each end of that joint.

11. Secure each roof panel to its respective front panel with two hinges, each placed 1" from an end of the plywood joint.

12. Cut the roof stops, which prevent the roof panels from dropping too low, to 24" in length. Using your adjustable square set for 13/16", mark a line along one face of each piece.

13. With your circular-saw blade set for 30°, rip the two roof stops along the marked lines.

14. Set the 3/4"-wide face of a roof stop on the front panel. The stop should be centered along the plywood edge, and its beveled edge should face up and toward the front panel's top edge. Fasten the stop to the plywood by driving 1-1/4" screws through the plywood and into the stop. Then repeat to fasten the other roof stop to the other front panel's inside face in the same way.

15. The mending plate is used to hold the two roof panels in position at the proper angle and is permanently fastened to one roof panel only. Fasten the plate to the inside face of either panel, near the pointed end farthest from the hinged edge. Locate one of the plate's mounting holes 2" from the plywood corner's pointed end and cen-

ROOF LATCH DETAIL

tered between the two adjacent edges. Then drive one of the mending plate's screws through the hole to secure the plate to the plywood.

16. Drive a screw into the identical position on the second roof panel's corner, but this time use a smaller screw, the head of which will fit easily through the mending plate's other mounting hole. Engaging the smaller screw in the mending plate secures the Fresh Market in set-up position.

17. Set the assembled Fresh Market upright on the floor or ground, closing the hinged front panels to an angle of approximately 110°. Handle the project carefully when you open it or fold it closed, or the two roof panels will flop about and damage the project or injure you. Lower

the roof panels until their adjacent edges are aligned and, using pliers, carefully bend the mending plate in its middle so that its shape matches that of the pair of roof panels. The mending plate's open hole should now slip over the screw you inserted in Step 16; if it doesn't, adjust the screw's location or the mending plate's angle so that the alignment is correct.

18. With the mending plate in place and properly fastened, join the two inside faces of the front panels by fastening each end of a 30" length of Jack chain to the inside face of a front panel. Use a 1" screw to fasten each end, locating the screws below the roof stops and above the windows so that the chain won't interfere with your young shopkeepers' activities. This chain "indexes" the open angle of the front panels and will make it easy to lower the roof panels into their correct positions.

19. Carefully lay out the 3/4" plywood countertop, using the dimensions given in the Countertop illustration. Mark 1"-radius corners as shown and, using your circular saw and jigsaw, cut the shape out. Finally, with your router and 3/8" rounding-over bit, round all arrises of the countertop except for those on the two edges that will contact the plywood front panels (see Step 20).

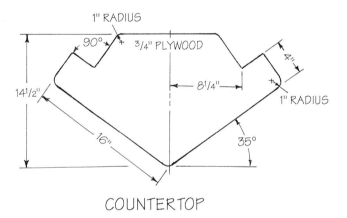

COUNTERTOP

20. The countertop fits on top of the center window's bottom edges and is prevented from tipping over by the bottoms of the two side stiles. Slide the countertop into place, checking to see that its square edges fit tightly against the plywood front panels. If they don't, you may need to remove a little wood from the bottom of each window stile so that the countertop fits underneath them.

21. Using your router setup, round any trim pieces that little hands might otherwise find too rough.

22. Sand all parts of the Fresh Market, including the interior. Belt sanders are ideal for smoothing spots where plywood edges and trim-piece edges don't quite align; hand sanding is the best alternative for tight corners where power sanders can't reach. Dust the parts off thoroughly.

23. Cut the two identical side poles, the top center pole, and the bottom center pole to length. Use your rasp or spokeshave to round the top ends of the side poles and both ends of the top center pole. Then sand the poles and dust them off.

24. To make a slot at one end of the top center pole, first secure the pole with its rounded end up. Then lay out a 5"-long line from the pole's top down its center. With your panel saw, carefully cut down through the line to create a 5"-deep slot. Repeat to cut slots into the rounded ends of the side poles.

25. Using sharp scissors, cut the nylon flag shapes in any pattern you like; the ends that attach to the posts should be 5" wide. To fasten the flags in place, slip their 5"-wide ends into the slots in the poles and drive three No. 18 x 3/4" brads through each pole and flag end.

26. Secure a side pole to the front face of a front panel, aligning it with the front panel's outermost edge. To fasten it in place, drive 1-1/4" deck screws, spaced approximately 6" apart, through the inside face of the plywood and into the pole. Repeat to fasten the second side pole to the opposite plywood front panel.

27. To attach the top center pole, position it against the end of the top rail on the left-hand front panel (as viewed from the front) and against the end of a center window stile; set its bottom end 1" below the center window's top. Then drive two 2-1/2" deck screws through the pole,

one into the rail and one into the stile.

28. Position the bottom center pole against the bottom rail of the center window and against the front bottom rail (both on the left-hand front panel). Fasten the pole in place as in Step 27.

29. Finish the Fresh Market in your choice of colors, priming carefully before you paint. For a project that will last for many years, coat any unpainted surfaces with water sealer.

Use your imagination (and cutoffs from your scrap bin) to design, fabricate, and finish a set of groceries. This one is sized to fit the Market Basket project shown on page 80 and includes basic food shapes ranging from moo juice and cereal boxes to hefty slices of cheddar cheese.

CUT LIST (for one set of eight shapes)

1	2" x 2" x 7-1/4"	Milk carton
1	2" x 2" x 3-1/2"	Butter carton
1	1-1/2" x 3-1/2" x 5"	Cereal box
1	1-1/2" x 3-1/2" x 2-1/4"	Cheese wedge
1	3/4" x 3-1/2" x 5"	Large packaged food
1	3/4" x 2" x 4"	Small packaged food
1	1-1/2" x 1-1/2" x 7"	Foil or plastic wrap
1	1-1/4" x 2-1/4" dowel	Canned beverage

HARDWARE AND SUPPLIES

Exterior alkyd primer
Alkyd enamel paint
Mineral spirits

SUGGESTED TOOLS

Layout tools
Backsaw
Coping saw
Circular saw
Orbital sander
1" paintbrush

TIP

■ Be especially cautious when you cut small parts with your circular saw (see Step 1). Wear safety glasses, guard against breakup and flying debris by securing the work firmly to your work surface, and keep the blade well clear of metal clamps.

INSTRUCTIONS

1. Using the illustrations as guides, first lay out the parts on scrap stock and cut them out with the type of saw that is safest and most appropriate.

2. Sand all the parts carefully, finishing them with 220-grit sandpaper. Then dust them thoroughly with a tack rag.

3. Finish the set in colors your kids will enjoy. To ensure a bright, long-lasting finish, begin with a coat of primer. If your children are still "chewers," as many toddlers are, use a transparent salad-bowl finish or another nontoxic finish instead.

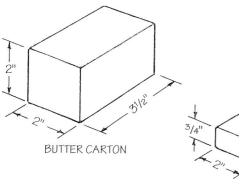

BUTTER CARTON

SMALL PACKAGED FOOD

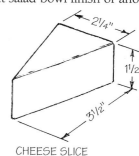

CHEESE SLICE

LARGE PACKAGED FOOD

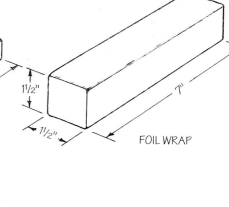

FOIL WRAP

GROCERY SET

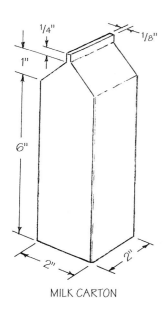

MILK CARTON

CEREAL BOX

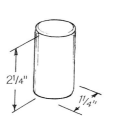

BEVERAGE CAN

Kids will love toting their store purchases home in this traditional market basket. Its small scale makes it an ideal project for involving your kids as apprentice builders.

CUT LIST

1	3/4" x 5-1/2" x 9-3/4"	Bottom (measured long point to long point)
2	3/4" x 5-1/2" x 5-3/4"	Ends (measured long point to short point)
2	3/4" x 1-1/4" x 11"	Handle supports
1	1-1/4" x 6" dowel	Handle
1	1/4" x 1-1/2" x 80" lattice	Slats (six; scribed to length)

HARDWARE AND SUPPLIES

4d casing nails (24)
1-1/2" deck screws (10)
3/4" deck screws (2)
Finishing materials as desired

SUGGESTED TOOLS

Layout tools
Claw hammer
Backsaw
No. 2 screwdriver
Circular saw
3/8" drill
Pilot bits to match screw sizes
No. 2 drive bit
Router
3/8" rounding-over bit
Orbital sander
Finishing tools as desired

INSTRUCTIONS

1. Set your circular saw for 20° and cut a bevel across one end of the 3/4" stock. Lay out the bottom by marking 9-3/4" from that bevel-cut end (long point to long point). Turn the board end-for-end and make a second bevel cut at the marked line. Keep in mind that the two bevel cuts on this piece should be mirror images of one another.

2. Using the bevel cut on the remaining 3/4" stock as a starting point, lay out and cut an end piece. The 5-3/4" length of this piece is measured from long point to short

point, and its bevel cuts should be identical. Refer to the illustration for help envisioning these cuts. Repeat to lay out and cut a second end piece exactly like the first one.

3. Using your drill and pilot bit, bore three pilot holes for 1-1/2" screws into the face of an end piece, 3/8" from the short point. Place one hole 2-3/4" from an edge and the other two holes 2" to either side of the first hole. Repeat to bore three holes in the other end piece.

4. Secure the bottom piece in an upright position. Align the long point of an end piece with the short point of the bottom piece and line up the edges of both parts. Fasten the pieces together by inserting three screws through the pilot-bored holes in the end piece. Repeat to secure the other end piece onto the opposite end of the bottom piece.

5. To determine the length of the first slat, set the ends-

MARKET BASKET

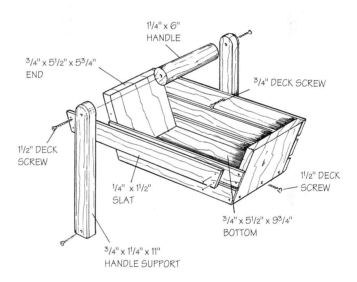

1¼" x 6"
HANDLE

³⁄₄" x 5¹⁄₂" x 5³⁄₄"
END

³⁄₄" DECK SCREW

1½" DECK
SCREW

¼" x 1¹⁄₂"
SLAT

³⁄₄" x 5¹⁄₂" x 9³⁄₄"
BOTTOM

1½" DECK
SCREW

³⁄₄" x 1¹⁄₄" x 11"
HANDLE SUPPORT

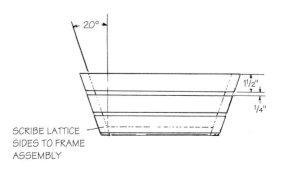

20°

1½"

¼"

SCRIBE LATTICE
SIDES TO FRAME
ASSEMBLY

and-bottom assembly on its side. Then align the lower edge of the 1-1/2" lattice stock with the lower edge of the bottom piece. Using the outside faces of the end pieces as guides, scribe the lattice for cutting.

6. Place the scribed lattice on top of some scrap wood and, using your backsaw, cut along the two angled scribe marks. Then scribe and saw an identical piece of lattice, using the angle-cut end of the lattice stock as one end of this second piece.

7. Set one of these two slats onto the assembly, aligning its short edge with the bottom's lower edge. Secure the slat by driving two 4d galvanized nails though it and into each end piece. Repeat to secure the other slat to the other side of the assembly.

8. Repeat Steps 5 through 7 to scribe, cut, and secure the two uppermost slats.

9. Set the lattice stock onto the assembly so that it's equally spaced between the two slats already secured; scribe the stock for cutting. Saw out this slat and secure it between the other two. Flip the assembly and repeat to scribe, cut, and fasten the last lattice slat.

10. Use your adjustable square and a pencil or marking knife to lay out two handle supports, each 3/4" x 1-1/4" x 11". Cut the two pieces to length with your circular saw.

11. Secure a handle support face up on your work surface. Using the 1-1/4" dowel stock as a guide, scribe a semicircular radius on one end of each handle support's face. Cut the radius on each piece with your coping saw.

12. With your router and 3/8" rounding-over bit, shape the arrises on the outer face of each handle support.

13. On the face of each handle support, bore a pilot hole 5/8" from the radiused end and centered at 5/8" across the face. Bore another centered pilot hole 3/8" from the square end of each support.

14. Use your backsaw to cut the 1-1/4" dowel stock to a 6" length.

15. Set the assembled basket on its side. Fasten the square end of each handle support to the center of a bottom lattice piece, using your drive bit to insert screws through the pilot-bored holes. (The square end of each support should be flush with the edge of a lattice slat.) Also install a pilot-bored 3/4" screw through the center of each top slat to secure the handle supports so that they're exactly perpendicular to the bottom.

16. After aligning the dowel handle between the handle supports, fasten it in place with two 1-1/2" screws.

17. Sand all parts of the basket thoroughly. Then remove the sanding debris with a tack rag and finish the project as you like.

Blackboards ● ALL AGES

This simple project will provide endless hours of fun for young artists. The boards are sized to fit the Fresh Market project shown on page 73, but they can be altered to suit your needs and mounted just about anywhere. They even work well as lap boards for artists on the go.

BLACKBOARD

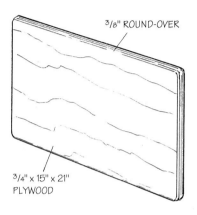

3/8" ROUND-OVER

3/4" x 15" x 21"
PLYWOOD

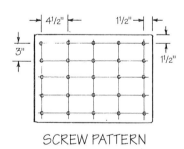

SCREW PATTERN

4¹/₂"   1¹/₂"

3"

1¹/₂"

CUT LIST (for two boards)
2   3/4" x 15" x 21" plywood   Blackboards

HARDWARE AND SUPPLIES
   1" deck screws (1 pound)
   Lightweight spackling compound
   Exterior alkyd primer
   Alkyd enamel "blackboard-finish" spray paint
   Mineral spirits
   Chalk

SUGGESTED TOOLS
   Layout tools
   No. 2 screwdriver
   Circular saw with plywood blade
   Router
   3/8" rounding-over bit
   3/8" drill
   Pilot bit to match screw size
   No. 2 drive bit
   Orbital sander
   Spackling knife

INSTRUCTIONS

1. To prevent chip-out, place the plywood on your work surface with its best face down. Then lay out two identical 15" x 21" blackboards on the top and saw them out carefully with your circular saw.

2. Secure one of the cut rectangles onto your work surface, turning its best face up. Use a router fitted with a 3/8" rounding-over bit to shape the four arrises. Repeat this step on the other rectangular piece.

3. Spackle any cracks or other defects on the best face of each piece. When the spackling compound has dried thoroughly, sand the faces flush and dust them off with a tack rag.

4. Prime all surfaces of both pieces and let the primer dry.

5. Set one of the blackboards on some old newspaper, out-of-doors and away from the wind. Following the directions on the spray can, apply a coat of finish to the best face and edges of the piece. Recoat after the first coat has dried; additional coats will result in a tougher blackboard.

6. To mount the blackboards on the Fresh Market project, first bore twenty-five pilot holes through the back of each panel of the Fresh Market. Space these holes as shown in the Screw Pattern illustration, locating them so that the blackboards can be secured to the panels approximately 5" below the window openings and 5" from each panel's outside edge. Fasten the boards in place with 1" screws.

7. Before the boards are used, coat their front surfaces by rubbing them with a piece of chalk turned on its side. Wipe off the excess chalk dust with a chalkboard eraser.

Setting
Up
House

CARRY-TABLE & CARRY-CHAIRS ● 4 AND UNDER 🏛

This colorful kid-sized furniture knocks down, stacks up, and goes anywhere kids go.

CUT LIST (for two chairs and one table)

2	3/4" x 13-1/2"-diameter plywood	Chair seat
4	3/4" x 12" x 12" plywood	Seat bases A and B
1	3/4" x 24"-diameter plywood	Tabletop
2	3/4" x 18" x 23" plywood	Table bases A and B
3	1/4" x 2" dowel	Index pins

HARDWARE AND SUPPLIES

Luggage catches (6)
Resin glue
Exterior alkyd primer
Alkyd enamel paint
Mineral spirits

SUGGESTED TOOLS

Layout tools
Panel saw
Backsaw
Chisel
Bench mallet
Compass
Pilot bit to match hardware screws
Screwdriver to fit hardware screws
Circular saw
Jigsaw
3/8" drill
1/4" brad-point bit
Orbital sander
1-1/2" paintbrush

TIP

■ Try a luggage supplier for the luggage catches.

INSTRUCTIONS

1. Begin by laying out the four 12" x 12" seat bases and the two 18" x 23" table bases; make sure the best side of the plywood stock faces down. Then use your circular saw to cut out each piece.

CARRY TABLE

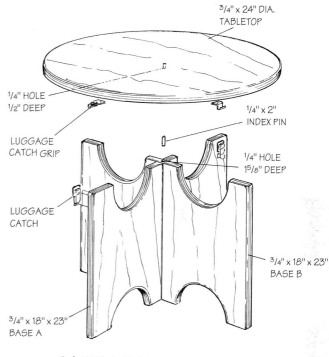

3/4" x 24" DIA. TABLETOP

1/4" HOLE 1/2" DEEP

1/4" x 2" INDEX PIN

LUGGAGE CATCH GRIP

1/4" HOLE 1⁵/₈" DEEP

LUGGAGE CATCH

3/4" x 18" x 23" BASE B

3/4" x 18" x 23" BASE A

CARRY CHAIR

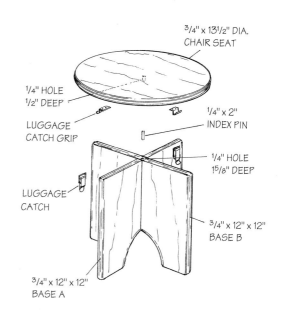

3/4" x 13¹/₂" DIA. CHAIR SEAT

1/4" HOLE 1/2" DEEP

LUGGAGE CATCH GRIP

1/4" x 2" INDEX PIN

1/4" HOLE 1⁵/₈" DEEP

LUGGAGE CATCH

3/4" x 12" x 12" BASE B

3/4" x 12" x 12" BASE A

2. Set a seat base face up on your work surface and lay out the pattern for the centered half-lap joint, as shown in the Base A illustration. Start the parallel cuts with your circular saw and finish

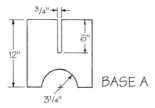

BASE A

them with a panel saw. Then remove the cutout by using a mallet and chisel. Repeat to remove identical cutouts from the other three seat bases.

3. Set a seat base face up on your work surface and mark a centerpoint on the arris that is opposite to the cutout. Then lay out a 6-1/2"-diameter semicircle, centering it at that point (refer to the Base A illustration). This semicircle will serve as a decorative cutout and needn't be exact.

4. Saw out the semicircle with your jigsaw. Repeat to lay out and cut an identical semicircle from one more seat base A.

5. Repeat Steps 3 and 4 with the two seat bases B, but on these pieces, lay out and cut the semicircles along the slotted cutout edges (see the Base B illustration).

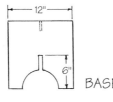

BASE B

6. Test-fit the A and B pieces together. If a joint is too tight for a child to disassemble, use a mallet and chisel to trim the cutouts. Label each pair of fitted parts.

7. Set a table-base piece face up on your work surface. Begin by laying out, sawing, and chiseling a 3/4" x 9" cutout from the face, as shown in the Base A illustration.

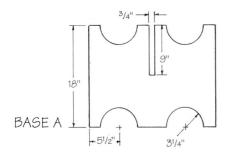

BASE A

8. The decorative semicircles on the table bases A and B are identical in size to those on the seat bases, but their locations are different. Measure and mark two points on the arrises of both long edges of one base piece; locate each point 5-1/2" from a corner. Using these points as centers for your compass, mark four 6-1/2"-diameter semicircles on the base's face, one on either side of the 3/4" x 6" cutout and two on the long edge above it.

9. Saw out the semicircles with your jigsaw. Make table base B by repeating Steps 7 and 8.

10. Test-fit the bases and make any necessary adjustments. Label the pieces A and B when you're done.

11. Lay out the two 13-1/2"-diameter chair seats and the single 24"-diameter tabletop on the plywood stock's face. Cut out the three pieces with your jigsaw.

12. Using your router and 3/8" rounding-over bit, shape the arrises of the chair seats, tabletop, and all bases, but omit the slotted cutouts and the base edges that will butt the chair seats and tabletop.

13. Lay out and bore a 1/4" hole, 1-5/8" deep, in the top (square) edge of all three part B pieces. Locate each hole 3/8" from an arris and center it between the adjacent edges of the base piece.

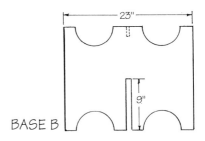

BASE B

14. Locate and bore a 1/4" hole, 1/2" deep, in the center of each top piece's bottom face.

15. Use your backsaw to cut three 2" lengths of 1/4" dowel. Then glue one end of each piece into each of the base B holes that you bored in Step 13. Round the free ends of all three fastened dowels until the holes in the top pieces fit easily over them.

16. Sand and dust off the various parts. Then prime them with exterior alkyd primer and paint them with two coats of alkyd enamel paint.

17. To secure the tops onto the bases, mount two luggage catches on each of the base pieces A and on the three tops. The larger, hinging parts of the catches mount on the bases near the top edges; these tighten onto the catches mounted on the undersides of the top pieces. Use a pilot bit and a screwdriver for the small screws that secure the catches.

18. Assemble the pairs of bases with their square edges facing up, set the top pieces on top of them, and tighten the catches. After demonstrating the assembly process for your kids, encourage them to store the project parts safely away when the weather turns stormy.

TOT LOUNGER

Small children enjoy furniture that's sized just for them. This knockdown lounger is also lightweight enough for youngsters to tote along on their next backyard vacation.

CUT LIST

1	3/4" x 11-1/4" x 18"	Seat
1	3/4" x 11-1/4" x 22"	Seat back
2	3/4" x 1-1/2" x 10-1/2"	Battens

HARDWARE AND SUPPLIES

1-1/4" deck screws (6)

SUGGESTED TOOLS

Layout tools	3/8" drill
Panel saw	2" Forstner bit
Bench mallet	Pilot bit to match screw size
Compass	No. 2 drive bit
Chisel	Router
No. 2 screwdriver	3/8" rounding-over bit
Circular saw	Orbital sander
Jigsaw	

TIPS

■ If you don't have a compass handy, use two cans (with 3" and 6" diameters respectively) to mark the radii at the corners of the seat and seat back.

■ Using cedar or another lightweight lumber for this project will make carrying the two chair parts easier for your small children.

■ If the chair feels "tippy," show your tot how to steady it while sitting down and getting up.

INSTRUCTIONS

1. Use your layout tools and circular saw to mark and cut the seat, seat back, and two battens to size, ripping the battens as necessary.

2. Lay out a 3/4" x 13/16" x 4-5/8" slot on the seat, as shown in the illustration. Note that one edge of the slot begins 9" from one end of the seat and is parallel to it.

3. Use your circular saw to begin the two parallel cuts and finish them with your panel saw. Remove the tongue from the slot by using your chisel and mallet.

4. Lay out and cut an identically-sized slot in the seat back, using the illustration and Steps 2 and 3 as a guide. This slot opens onto a long side but its lower edge is located just 4-1/4" from an end of the seat back.

5. Test-fit the two slotted parts to get a feel for the shape of the chair. Then trim the joint until the parts slide together easily.

6. With the seat and seat back facing up, lay out a radius at each corner of each piece, as shown in the illustrations. Use a compass or a can of appropriate diameter to do this job.

7. Cut the radii to shape with your jigsaw.

8. Lay out and bore a 2" hole in each piece, using the illustration as your guide. Each hole is centered 2" from a long edge of a seat piece.

9. Using your router and 3/8" rounding-over bit, round all arrises on both pieces, except for the arrises on the slots.

10. Set a batten face up for boring. Then lay out and bore three 1-1/4" pilot holes, 4-1/2" apart, along the center of its face. Repeat to bore identical holes in the second batten.

11. Using the illustrations as guides, center and secure a batten face-to-face with each seat piece; align the batten edges with one edge of each slot. Fasten the battens in place with three 1-1/4" deck screws.

12. Sand the two seat assemblies lightly, dust them off, and seal them with two coats of water seal. Then show your child how the pieces fit together to make a comfortable chair.

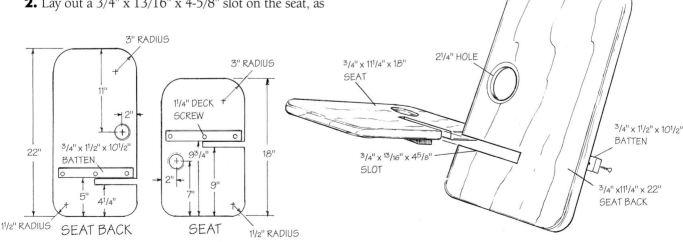

More experienced builders will have as much fun tackling this heirloom-quality post-and-beam playhouse as their children will have playing in it. The project's substantial construction and weather-resistant materials ensure years of exciting play, and its handsome appearance will be appreciated by the "old folks" as well. To build in the most fun, be sure to include the related projects; instructions for these begin on page 99.

CUT LIST

2	1-1/2" x 3-1/2" x 96"	Base sides
5	1-1/2" x 3-1/2" x 45"	Base braces
1	5/8" x 48" x 96" plywood	Floor
2	3-1/2" x 3-1/2" x 91"	Side plates
1	3-1/2" x 3-1/2" x 48"	Rear plate
6	3-1/2" x 3-1/2" x 52"	Posts
1	3-1/2" x 3-1/2" x 95"	Ridge beam
2	3-1/2" x 3-1/2" x 95"	Top plate
10	3-1/2" x 3-1/2" x 38"	Rafters
6	1-1/2" x 1-1/2" x 48"	Post battens
2	1-1/2" x 1-1/2" x 50-1/4"	Front corner battens
5	1-1/2" x 1-1/2" x 38"	Top and bottom battens
2	1-1/2" x 1-1/2" x 27-1/2"	Short rafter battens
2	1-1/2" x 1-1/2" x 29"	Long rafter battens
1	1-1/2" x 1-1/2" x 5-1/2"	Short front panel batten
1	1-1/2" x 1-1/2" x 17-1/2"	Long front panel batten
2	1-1/2" x 1-1/2" x 48-1/2"	Long door battens
1	1-1/2" x 1-1/2" x 21"	Short door batten
1	1/2" x 44-1/2" x 74-1/4" plywood	Front panel
1	1/2" x 44-1/2" x 70-3/4" plywood	Back panel
2	1/2" x 41" x 48" plywood	Side panels
1	1/2" x 41" x 48" plywood	Roof panel A
1	1/2" x 41-1/2" x 48" plywood	Roof panel B
2	3/4" x 3-1/2" x 34-1/2"	Trim stiles A
2	3/4" x 3-1/2" x 35-1/4"	Trim stiles B
4	3/4" x 3-1/2" x 48"	Trim rails
4	3/4" x 3-1/2" x 15"	Window stiles
4	3/4" x 3-1/2" x 17"	Window rails
6	1-1/2" x 1-1/2" x 9-3/4"	Short half-lap muntins; top and bottom window battens
4	1-1/2" x 1-1/2" x 22"	Side window battens
2	1-1/2" x 1-1/2" x 14-3/4"	Long half-lap muntins
1	1/2" x 18" x 20"	Top door panel
1	1/2" x 18" x 30"	Bottom door panel
1	3/4" x 3-1/2" x 25"	Top door rail
4	3/4" x 3-1/2" x 11"	Door rails
2	3/4" x 3-1/2" x 20"	Top door stiles
2	3/4" x 3-1/2" x 30"	Bottom door stiles
2	3/4" x 3-1/2" x 50"	Side door stiles
2	3/4" x 3-1/4" x 50"	Long door stops
1	3/4" x 3-1/4" x 16-1/2"	Short door stop
2	1-1/2" x 3-1/2" x 39-1/2"	Top and bottom porch rails
20	1-1/2" x 1-1/2" x 20"	Porch stiles

HARDWARE AND SUPPLIES

1" deck screws (1 pound)
2" deck screws (7)
2-1/2" deck screws (1 pound)
1-1/4" deck screws (3 pounds)
1/4" x 2-1/2" lag screws with washers (2)
1/4" x 4-1/2" lag screws with washers (14)
1/4" x 5" lag screws with washers (20)
6d casing nails (1 pound)
8d casing nails (1 pound)
4d casing nails (20)
2" x 2-1/2" butt hinges with screws (4)
6" x 48" aluminum flashing
Construction adhesive
Water sealer
Handle set (1)

SUGGESTED TOOLS

Layout tools
Claw hammer
Caulking gun
Sledge hammer
Panel saw
Backsaw
Coping saw
Ratchet wrench with 7/16" socket
Flat rasp
Nos. 1 and 2 screwdrivers
No. 2 drive bit
Bench mallet
Chisels
Tin snips
Circular saw
Jigsaw
3/8" drill
7/8" Forstner bit
1/4" brad-point bit
Pilot bits to match screw sizes
Router
3/8" rounding-over bit
Orbital sander
3" paintbrush

TIPS

- If you wish, larger roof pieces may be used to cover the entire structure, including the porch.
- The completed cottage weighs quite a bit, but it can be disassembled when you want to change its location. To maintain it as a knockdown project, avoid gluing or otherwise fastening parts together except where noted.

In this project:

- The word *timber* always refers to pieces cut from 3-1/2" x 3-1/2" stock.
- All half-lap joints are 1-3/4" deep and 3-1/2" long.
- The bore for every lag screw consists of two parts: a 7/8"-diameter, 1/2"-deep counterbore that will hide the lag screw's head and washer safely below the surface; and a 1/4" pilot hole through the center of the counterbore. (Pilot bore only the counterbored timber; drive the lag screw's tip into the second timber by starting it with a hammer tap and complete the assembly with your ratchet wrench.)

INSTRUCTIONS

1. To build the base, first cut the two base sides and the five base braces to the lengths given in the Cut List. Set the base parts on edge and assemble a framework by placing two braces between the two base sides, flush with the sides' ends. (Work on a large, flat surface.) Secure each joint with two 2-1/2" deck screws driven through the outside face of the base side. Then fasten the other three braces inside the framework, spacing them at equal distances and butting their ends against the inside faces of the base sides.

2. To square the assembly, stretch your tape measure across both diagonals; adjust the assembly until both readings are identical. Now, with your caulking gun, run a 3/16" bead of construction adhesive along the top edges of the framework. Then get a helper to give you a hand setting the plywood floor onto the gluey edges. Square the edges and secure the floor to the framework with 6d casing nails spaced 6" apart. Sand the assembly and finish it with exterior-grade materials of your choice.

3. Cut the two side-plate timbers to 91" in length.

4. Set a side plate with one face up and lay out an open half-lap joint, 1-3/4" deep and 3-1/2" long, at one end. (The word *open* indicates that the cutout is located at the end of a timber. For more information on half-lap joints, see page 24.) Saw the face cut with a circular saw set at a 1-3/4" depth; make the end cut with your backsaw or panel saw.

FRAME CONSTRUCTION

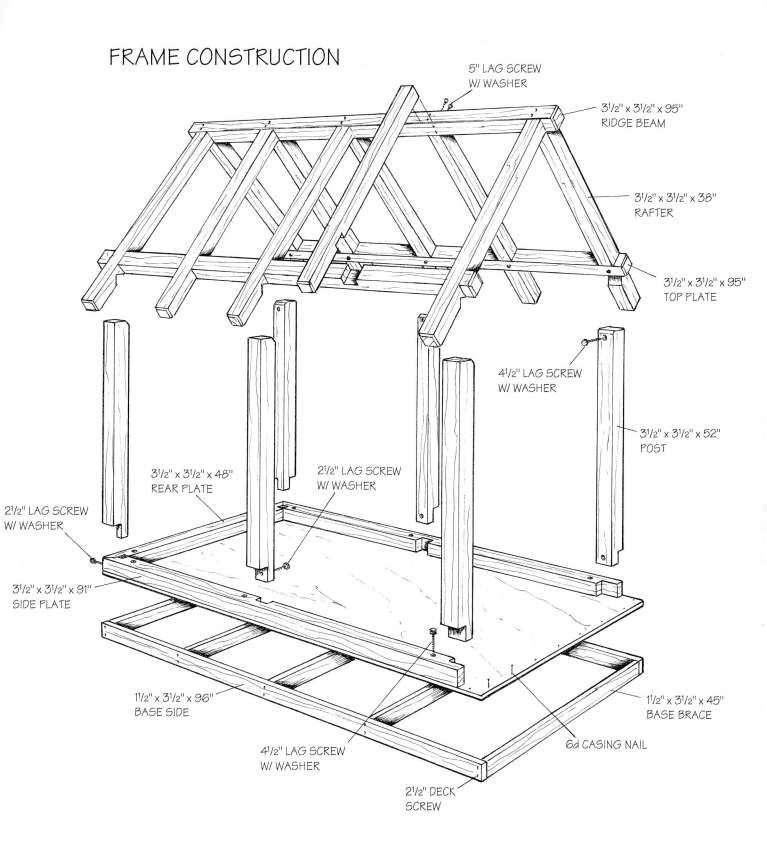

5" LAG SCREW
W/ WASHER

3½" x 3½" x 95"
RIDGE BEAM

3½" x 3½" x 38"
RAFTER

3½" x 3½" x 95"
TOP PLATE

4½" LAG SCREW
W/ WASHER

3½" x 3½" x 52"
POST

3½" x 3½" x 48"
REAR PLATE

2½" LAG SCREW
W/ WASHER

2½" LAG SCREW
W/ WASHER

3½" x 3½" x 91"
SIDE PLATE

1½" x 3½" x 96"
BASE SIDE

1½" x 3½" x 45"
BASE BRACE

6d CASING NAIL

4½" LAG SCREW
W/ WASHER

2½" DECK
SCREW

5. Position the side plate so that the first half-lap joint faces up. To locate a *closed* half-lap joint (a joint that lies at some distance from an end) near the middle of the side plate and on the same face, set your tape measure's hook over the face cut you made and mark the top face at 39-1/2" and 43".

6. Square across the face at both points. Then, on the face nearest to you, square down 1-3/4" from both marks. With a circular saw set for a 1-3/4" cutting depth, cut the top face's squared lines to define the half-lap joint's width.

7. Flip the timber onto an adjacent side. Using your bench mallet and chisel, carefully remove the wood from the cutout. With an adjustable square, check the sides and bottom of the half-lap to be certain they're square.

8. The last, more complex joint in the side plate is located at its remaining square end (see the Corner Joint

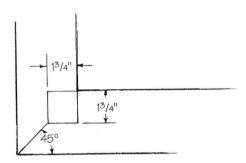

CORNER JOINT DETAIL

Detail). First, with the side plate's half-lap joints facing up, mark a line parallel with the end and 3-1/2" from it. Make a 1-3/4"-deep cut on that line.

9. Turn the timber a quarter-turn toward you. Mark a centered line from the timber's end to the bottom of the 1-3/4" cut. Cut along this line with your backsaw and remove the block of waste.

10. Turn the timber another quarter-turn toward you. Set your circular saw for 45° and maximum depth. With the saw's table on the top face and using the end of the top face as your guideline, saw a 45° cut into the end of the side plate and remove the triangular block of waste. Repeat Steps 4 through 10 to cut three identical joints into the other side plate.

11. Cut the rear-plate timber to 48" in length. Then complete Steps 8 through 10 to cut a corner joint into each end of it. Locate both joints on the same face.

12. Secure a side plate for boring, with its joints facing away from you. Next, on the top face, 5/8" from the face

nearest you, bore three lag-screw counterbores and pilot holes; locate each of two holes 6" from an end and the third hole 49" from the end of the open half-lap joint. Repeat to counterbore the other side plate, but do so in reversed ("mirror") fashion.

13. Bore two lag-screw counterbores and pilot holes into the rear plate, orienting the plate as in Step 12. Locate the center of each hole 6" from a corner joint's pointed end and 5/8" from the face nearest you.

14. Set the rear plate onto the plywood floor so that its 48"-long outside face aligns with the floor's 48" end. Set a 4-1/2" lag screw with washer into each counterbore. Tap the screws lightly with a claw hammer to start them into the plywood below and then tighten them with your ratchet wrench.

15. Set a side plate's outside edge along the 96" edge of the floor, so that its corner joint meets the rear plate's corner joint at the rear corner of the floor. Install three lag screws with washers in the counterbores. Repeat to install the other side plate so that its half-lap joints face those of the first side plate.

16. Cut each of the six post timbers to 52" in length.

17. With a post positioned face up, bore a lag-screw hole into the face, 1-1/4" from one end and centered across the 3-1/2" face. Repeat with the other five posts.

18. Cut an open half-lap joint at one end of four of the posts (the two front posts and the two middle posts). The joints should be cut at the opposite end from the holes bored in Step 17.

19. To chamfer the inside top arris of a front post, first secure a post with its joint facing down and square a line on the top face, 3/4" from the end opposite to the joint. Use a circular saw set at 45° to cut a bevel at that line. Repeat to chamfer these arrises on every post.

20. Through the inside face of each front and middle post, bore a lag-screw hole centered just above the half-lap cutout, 1-3/4" from an adjacent face and from the end.

21. Secure one of the uncut rear posts with its unbored end facing up. To lay out a tenon on that end, first square two perpendicular lines across the center of the end. Then square four lines around the four faces of the post, locating each line 3-1/2" from the marked end and parallel to it. Position the post's end for layout so that the counterbore at the other end will face inside the cottage when assembled. Check the illustration to get a sense of how the tenon is oriented.

22. Use your backsaw (or panel saw) to cut down through both lines on the end, stopping the cuts at the

3-1/2" marks on the faces. Then cut halfway through the timber along two adjacent 3-1/2" lines on the face so as to leave a 1-3/4" x 1-3/4" x 3-1/2" tenon remaining at one corner of the post's end. Remove the last bits of waste with a mallet and chisel. Repeat Steps 21 and 22 to create a tenon on the other rear post.

23. Test-fit both tenons into the corner joints formed by the back and side plates, trimming them with your chisel until they fit nicely and matching the joint-and-tenon pairs so that they'll line up correctly in Step 25.

24. Remove both rear posts. In the outside face of the rear plate, counterbore for two lag screws; center each hole 2-5/8" from an end and 1-3/4" from the top face.

25. Replace the rear-post tenons in the corner joints and secure them in place with 2-1/2" lag screws with washers.

26. Secure the lapped ends of the middle and front posts to the side plate's half-lap joints by installing 2-1/2" lag screws in their counterbores.

27. Cut the ridge-beam timber and the two top-plate timbers to 95" in length. Also cut the ten rafter timbers to 38" in length.

28. Set a rafter face up. Lay out and cut a closed half-lap joint, centered 9-1/2" from the rafter's end. Repeat to cut identical closed half-lap joints in all the rafters.

29. To lay out the V-joint rafter cutouts into which the upright posts will fit, first position one rafter with its half-lap joint facing up. Set your circular saw's table to 45° and its blade depth to 2-3/8". (Test-cut a scrap to be sure the depth is adjusted correctly.) Make one cut across the grain, aligning it with the edge of the half-lap joint; make another cut across the grain, 3-1/2" from the first, to free the triangular waste. Repeat to cut V-joints into five more of the ten rafters.

30. To chamfer one end of each rafter, bevel-cut each arris on the end nearest the half-lap joint.

31. Set a top plate face up. Lay out five closed half-lap joints along the face; center these 3-3/4", 25-1/4", 46-3/4", 69", and 91-1/4" from one end. Saw and chisel out the joints.

32. Turn the top plate so that its joints face down. Lay out and bore five counterbores for lag screws, each centered directly over the back of a cutout joint. Repeat Steps 31 and 32 to make five half-lap joints and five counterbores in the other top plate.

33. Measuring from an end, mark one face of the ridge beam at 4-7/8", 26-3/8", 47-7/8," 70-1/8", and 92-3/8". Then, measuring from the same end, lay out marks on an adjacent face at 2-5/8", 24-1/8", 45-5/8", 67-7/8", and 90-1/8". Square across the layout marks on each face.

34. Mark and bore a pair of counterbores on each line squared in the last step, centering each hole 3/4" from an arris. (You may need a bit extension to bore through the entire thickness of the ridge beam.) Note that the paired holes on one face of the ridge beam are offset from those on the other face so that the holes won't interfere with one another.

35. Chamfer the ends of the ridge beam and the two top plates.

36. Using 2-1/2" lag screws with washers, fasten five rafters to one top plate. Begin at one end with a V-jointed rafter and then alternate rafters without and with V-joints, aligning each rafter in the same direction. Repeat to secure a second top-plate-and-rafter assembly.

37. To form the roof structure, bolt the adjacent (unbored) faces of the ridge beam to the square ends of both assemblies, using paired 5" lag screws so that the rafters' square ends align along the ridge beam exactly as their half-laps align along the top plates.

38. Get several friends to help you raise the roof! First, to tie the six posts together (each in plumb position), use 6d casing nails to tack some long scrap pieces of lumber across and around the posts' exteriors. Have 4-1/2" lag screws with washers handy; assign someone to tighten them in place when the roof is raised. Then, with at least one individual at each corner, lift the roof into position and place each rafter's V-joint cutout onto the appropriate post top. Secure the parts with the lag screws. Then remove the scrap wood.

39. To support the plywood front, back, and sides, 1-1/2" x 1-1/2" battens are fastened to various timbers and to the floor. Examine the illustrations that show how these battens are applied and then cut the battens to the lengths in the Cut List. (Note that in the Roof and Wall Construction illustration on the next page, the cottage is portrayed with its tenon-cut rear posts in the foreground; the porch—or front—is shown at the back.)

40. Bore pilot holes for 2-1/2" deck screws, spaced approximately 6" apart, through the battens that will be fastened along the inside arrises of the timbers that describe the enclosed portion of the cottage. Then fasten the battens to the timbers. (Ignore the long and short front-panel battens for the time being.)

41. Using a router with a 3/8" rounding-over bit, round any arrises on the frame that will be within reach of your youngsters' hands. On edges the router can't reach, use a rasp instead. Then sand the entire assembly well.

ROOF AND WALL CONSTRUCTION

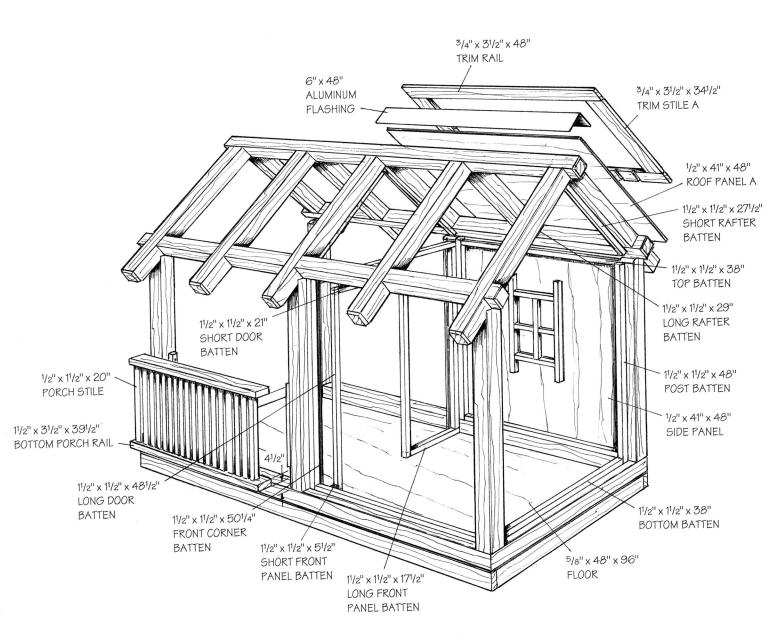

3/4" x 3½" x 48"
TRIM RAIL

6" x 48"
ALUMINUM
FLASHING

3/4" x 3½" x 34½"
TRIM STILE A

½" x 41" x 48"
ROOF PANEL A

1½" x 1½" x 27½"
SHORT RAFTER
BATTEN

1½" x 1½" x 38"
TOP BATTEN

1½" x 1½" x 29"
LONG RAFTER
BATTEN

1½" x 1½" x 21"
SHORT DOOR
BATTEN

½" x 1½" x 20"
PORCH STILE

1½" x 1½" x 48"
POST BATTEN

½" x 41" x 48"
SIDE PANEL

1½" x 3½" x 39½"
BOTTOM PORCH RAIL

1½" x 1½" x 48½"
LONG DOOR
BATTEN

4½"

1½" x 1½" x 38"
BOTTOM BATTEN

1½" x 1½" x 50¼"
FRONT CORNER
BATTEN

1½" x 1½" x 5½"
SHORT FRONT
PANEL BATTEN

1½" x 1½" x 17½"
LONG FRONT
PANEL BATTEN

5/8" x 48" x 96"
FLOOR

42. Using the three Panel illustrations as guides, cut the plywood front, back, and two sides. Test-fit these wall parts where they belong and trim any edges as necessary. Sand the parts (including their edges) well.

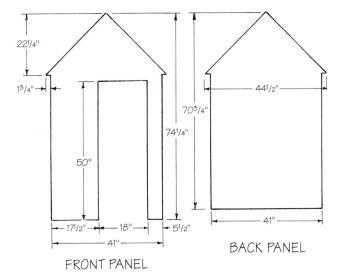

FRONT PANEL

BACK PANEL

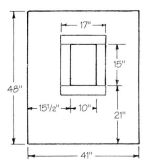

SIDE PANEL

43. Secure the window battens around the window cutouts as shown in the Window Detail, locating them so that each one overlaps the window's edge by 1/8" and fastening them in place with 1-1/4" deck screws spaced approximately 6" apart. Cut the half-lapped muntins and fasten them in place with pilot-bored 2-1/2" deck screws driven through the outermost muntins. Then fasten the long and short front-panel battens to the inside face of the front panel so that the edge of each batten lines up with the appropriate bottom edge of the

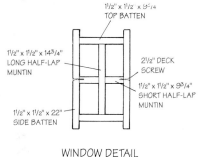

1½" x 1½" x 9¼"
TOP BATTEN

1½" x 1½" x 14¾"
LONG HALF-LAP
MUNTIN

2½" DECK
SCREW

1½" x 1½" x 9¾"
SHORT HALF-LAP
MUNTIN

1½" x 1½" x 22"
SIDE BATTEN

WINDOW DETAIL

panel. Use 1-1/4" pilot-bored deck screws driven through the outer face of the plywood to secure each piece.

44. Finish all sides and edges of the plywood pieces with any exterior-grade materials. When the pieces are dry, fasten them to the mounted battens in the cottage's interior, using piloted 1-1/4" deck screws spaced approximately 6" apart. (The front panel's short and long battens attach to the floor with 2" deck screws spaced in typical fashion.)

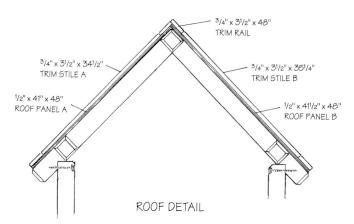

¾" x 3½" x 48"
TRIM RAIL

¾" x 3½" x 34½"
TRIM STILE A

¾" x 3½" x 35¼"
TRIM STILE B

½" x 41" x 48"
ROOF PANEL A

½" x 41½" x 48"
ROOF PANEL B

ROOF DETAIL

45. Saw out the two plywood roof panels. Then study the Roof Detail. Place the panels on the roof timbers above the front, back, and side panels with the 48" edges at the top and bottom; Panel B should overlap the top edge of Panel A at the roof's peak. Align the outside edges of the panels with the outside faces of the rafters. Using 1-1/4" deck screws spaced 6" apart, fasten the panels to the timbers.

46. Use your tin snips to cut a piece of flashing to 6" x 48". Then fold the piece neatly in half along its longest dimension. Set the flashing along the peak of the ridge beam, over the roof panels, lining up its ends with the outside faces of the rafters.

47. Saw the eight trim stiles and rails to length. Using the Roof Detail as a guide, position a rail at the top of panel A so that it covers the joint between panels A and B and its edge lines up with the outer face of roof panel B. Secure the rail in place with 1-1/4" screws. Then fasten another rail along the peak, lapping it over the first rail as shown in the illustration.

48. Attach the A and B stiles to the appropriate roof panels; align their edges with the panels' sloping edges and make sure one end of each stile butts the edge of a rail. Finally, attach the two remaining rails along the bottom edges of the panels, aligning them with the stiles' outer edges.

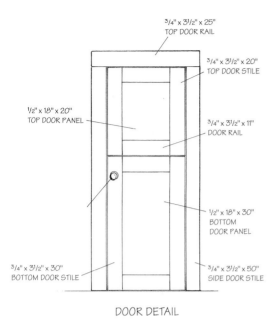

³/₄" x 3¹/₂" x 25"
TOP DOOR RAIL

³/₄" x 3¹/₂" x 20"
TOP DOOR STILE

¹/₂" x 18" x 20"
TOP DOOR PANEL

³/₄" x 3¹/₂" x 11"
DOOR RAIL

¹/₂" x 18" x 30"
BOTTOM
DOOR PANEL

³/₄" x 3¹/₂" x 30"
BOTTOM DOOR STILE

³/₄" x 3¹/₂" x 50"
SIDE DOOR STILE

DOOR DETAIL

49. Cut the door parts to the sizes specified in the Cut List.

50. Using the Door Detail as a guide, assemble the two-part door from the top and bottom door panels, the four stiles, and the four rails. Secure the stiles and rails to the panels with 1" screws driven from the inside of the plywood.

51. Mount two butt hinges at the inside edges of each door. Then mount the doors onto the battened plywood edges of the doorway so that there is a uniform margin between them and the edges of the door. Install the handle set in the bottom door according to the product's instructions and mount the sliding bolt's two parts on the doors' inside faces so that they fasten both doors together when the doors are closed. (Hinge the door so that it opens to the right as you face the front panel.) Then fasten the top door rail and two side door stiles in place, securing them with 2-1/2" deck screws driven through the inside faces of the long and short door battens.

52. Cut the door-stop pieces to size and mount them onto the doorway battens with 4d casing nails so that they butt the inside face of the door when it's closed. (These stops are installed in a similar fashion to those in the door openings of your home.) The short door stop mounts on the top, between the two long door stops.

53. Saw the window stiles and rails to size. Apply them around the outside of the window opening with 2-1/2" screws driven through the inside faces of the window battens.

54. To build the porch railing, begin by cutting the railing parts to the lengths in the Cut List. Then position

eighteen of the twenty stiles between the bottom and top rails. Set the first and last stiles 2" from the rails' ends, centering them across the width of each rail; space the remaining sixteen stiles 1/2" apart. Drive two 8d casing nails through each rail-and-stile joint, placing the nails at diagonals through the rails.

55. Center the remaining two stiles on opposing faces of the middle and front posts. Position the bottom end of each one 4-1/2" above the bottom plate and use three 2-1/2" deck screws to secure each end stile in place.

56. Slide the railing assembly onto the two attached end stiles, aligning the edges of the rails with the posts at each end. Fasten the assembly to the end stiles with 8d casing nails. (You may need to toe-nail the assembly at the bottom two joints.)

57. Finish the wooden parts with water sealer. Recoat from time to time to keep your Cozy Cottage looking great.

Window Boxes

These easy add-ons really dress up your Cozy Cottage.

WINDOW BOX

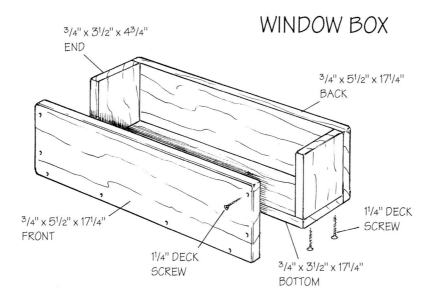

3/4" x 3-1/2" x 4-3/4"
END

3/4" x 5-1/2" x 17-1/4"
BACK

3/4" x 5-1/2" x 17-1/4"
FRONT

1-1/4" DECK
SCREW

1-1/4" DECK
SCREW

3/4" x 3-1/2" x 17-1/4"
BOTTOM

CUT LIST (for one box)

2	3/4" x 3-1/2" x 4-3/4"	Ends
2	3/4" x 5-1/2" x 17-1/4"	Front and back
1	3/4" x 3-1/2" x 17-1/4"	Bottom

HARDWARE AND SUPPLIES

1-1/4" deck screws (16)
2-1/2" deck screws (5)
Water sealer

SUGGESTED TOOLS

Layout tools
No. 2 screwdriver
Circular saw
3/8" drill
3/8" brad-point bit
Pilot bits to match screw sizes
No. 2 drive bit
Router
3/8" rounding-over bit
Orbital sander

TIP

■ Each window box is centered and mounted below a window, replacing the bottom window rail and butting up to the bottom ends of the window stiles.

INSTRUCTIONS

1. Begin by laying out and cutting the parts to length.

2. Bore four equally spaced pilot holes for 1-1/4" screws, 3/8" from one edge of the front piece. Repeat with the back piece and then fasten both pieces to the bottom piece as shown in the illustration.

3. Fit an end piece into each open end of the U-shape formed by the front, back, and bottom. Fasten each joint securely with two pilot-bored 1-1/4" deck screws.

4. Set the box so that the open side faces down. Use your 3/8" brad-point bit and drill to bore a drain hole near each end of the bottom piece's face.

5. To protect little hands against splinters, round all the arrises except those on the back piece.

6. Sand the assembly and wipe off the sanding debris.

7. Hold the box firmly below the window opening while you bore five pilot holes for 2-1/2" screws from the inside. Bore three of these holes through the bottom window batten, spacing them at equal distances, and one hole through each side batten, 3/4" from the batten's bottom end. Fasten the box in place with five 2-1/2" deck screws.

8. Finish your Window Box with two coats of water sealer. Then help your kids fill it with potting soil and seedlings.

Porch Swing

This lovely swing will be just as satisfying to friends who love sharing their time together as it will be to the child who enjoys daydreaming alone. Scaled to fit the Cozy Cottage project, it also works well when it's suspended from any substantial support such as a roof timber or a tree limb.

CUT LIST

1	1-1/2" x 1-1/2" x 28"	Top rail
1	1-1/2" x 1-1/2" x 28"	Middle rail
1	1-1/2" x 3-1/2" x 25"	Bottom rail
1	1-1/2" x 1-1/2" x 25"	Front rail
14	1-1/2" x 1-1/2" x 8-3/4"	Stiles
2	1-1/2" x 1-1/2" x 12-1/2"	Back supports
2	1-1/2" x 5-1/2" x 12"	Side supports
2	3/4" x 3-1/2" x 13"	Armrests
2	1-1/2" x 1-1/2" x 10-1/2"	Seat supports
6	3/4" x 1-1/2" x 28"	Seat slats

SUGGESTED TOOLS

Layout tools	Jigsaw
Compass	Router
Claw hammer	3/8" rounding-over bit
Nail set	3/8" drill
Screwdriver	3/16" brad-point bit
Slip-joint pliers	Pilot bits to match screw sizes
Backsaw	No. 2 drive bit
Hacksaw	Orbital sander
Circular saw	

PORCH SWING

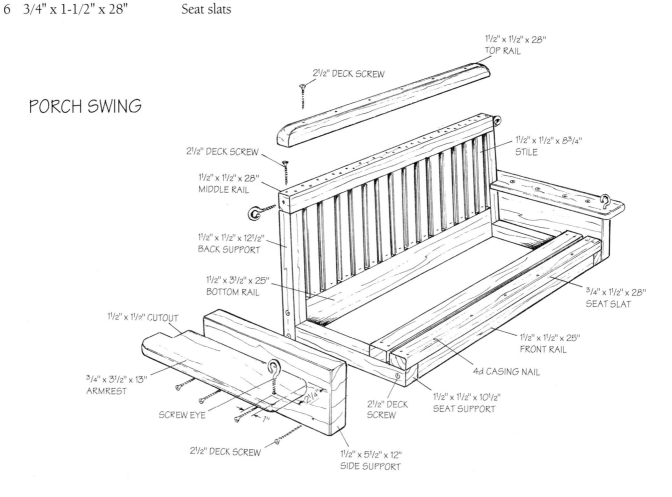

HARDWARE AND SUPPLIES

2-1/2" deck screws (2 pounds)
1-1/2" deck screws (8)
6' of double-loop chain; size 2/0
3/16" repair links (8)
4d casing nails (30)
6d casing nails (28)
Screw eyes; wire size 3 (6)

TIPS

- The Hardware and Supplies list includes hardware for mounting the swing to the Cozy Cottage's top plate. You may need longer pieces of chain and different hardware for different mounting applications.

- If 2/0 double-loop chain isn't available, any chain with a load test of at least 150 pounds is acceptable.

INSTRUCTIONS

1. Begin by laying out and cutting to length the parts listed in the Cut List. Label or otherwise organize the parts carefully to avoid assembly problems.

2. To assemble the swing's backrest, first position a back support at each end of the bottom rail; the bottom ends of the supports should be flush with the bottom edge of the rail. Then fasten the supports in place with two 2-1/2" deck screws driven through each support and into the end of the rail.

3. Position the middle rail to span the top ends of the two back supports. Align the rail's ends with the outermost edges of the supports and secure each joint with two 2-1/2" screws driven at a diagonal through the rail (see the illustration).

4. Position the fourteen stiles at equal distances from one another inside the backrest assembly. Fasten each stile in place by driving two 2-1/2" screws through the top of the middle rail and into the stile's end.

5. To secure the bottom end of each stile, toe-nail a 6d nail into each opposing face of a stile and on into the bottom rail.

6. Align the top rail on the middle rail so that the ends of both pieces are flush. Fasten the rails together with 2-1/2" screws driven at 5" intervals.

7. Set the backrest assembly flat and mark 1-1/2" radii at the two upper corners of the top rail. Cut the radii with your jigsaw.

8. Align the face of each 1-1/2" x 5-1/2" x 12" side support so as to form a right angle; the edges and ends should be flush. Fasten the side supports in place with two 2-1/2" screws.

9. Begin the seat assembly by setting the two 1-1/2" x 1-1/2" x 10-1/2" seat supports with their outside faces 28" apart. The seat slats span the two supports and are spaced at equal distances from one another. Position each slat in turn, securing it to the supports' faces with two 4d casing nails at each joint.

10. Place the front rail between the two seat supports, aligning it with the front seat slat. Secure the front rail in place with a 2-1/2" screw at each end and 4d casing nails driven through the front seat slat's face and into the front rail at 5" intervals.

11. Round the arris of the front slat with your router setup.

12. Referring to the illustration, position the seat assembly inside the side supports. Secure each end of the seat assembly with four equally spaced 2-1/2" screws driven through the side support and into the seat support.

13. Secure an armrest face up and lay out a 1-1/2" x 1-1/2" square cutout at one corner; use your backsaw to remove the waste. Repeat to lay out and cut the other armrest.

14. Round all arrises of the armrests except for the square-shaped cutouts and the ends where the cutouts are located.

15. Place each armrest onto the top edge of a side support so that its cutout wraps neatly around two adjacent faces of a back support. Secure the armrests to the side supports, using four equally spaced 1-1/2" screws on each side of the bench; drive these through the rests and into the supports.

16. Sand all parts of the porch swing carefully, wiping off the sanding debris.

17. Bore four 3/16"-diameter, 1-1/4"-deep holes for screw eyes into the four locations pictured in the illustration. Center two holes at the ends of the middle rail; locate the other two 1" from the front end of each armrest and 2-1/4" from its inside edges. Use your slip-joint pliers to install a screw eye into each bore-hole.

18. Finish the porch swing with two coats of water sealer and let it dry thoroughly.

19. The completed swing is hung from an overhead support with size 2/0 double-loop chain. For installation beneath the Cozy Cottage's top-plate timber, use your hacksaw to cut paired pieces of chain in three lengths as follows: 3, 4, and 10 double links—5", 7", and 22-3/4", respectively—for a total of six lengths.

20. Fasten a repair link to each screw eye. Then fasten the 5" lengths to the armrests' screw eyes and the 7" pieces to the middle support's screw eyes. Join the free ends of each pair of pieces together with repair links. Finally, connect a 22-3/4" length to each of the last two repair links you installed. The result, when the lengths of connected chain are stretched out, should resemble an upside-down Y above each armrest.

21. Using the installation method described in Step 17, insert the two remaining screw eyes into the underside of the cottage's top plate, spacing them the same distance apart as the screw eyes at opposite ends of the swing. After connecting a repair link to each screw eye, hang the swing's 22-3/4" chain lengths from them. Check that the swing hangs level across its front and that the seat is fixed at a height appropriate for your children. To adjust the incline of the swing's seat and backrest, just rearrange the links where the three lengths of chain come together at each side.

WINDOWPANE

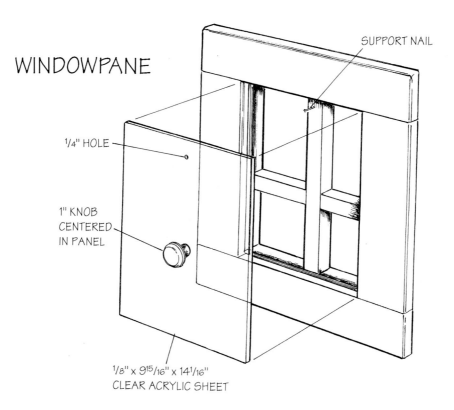

SUPPORT NAIL

1/4" HOLE

1" KNOB
CENTERED
IN PANEL

1/8" x 9¹⁵/₁₆" x 14¹/₁₆"
CLEAR ACRYLIC SHEET

These easy-to-build windowpanes help keep the elements out of your Cozy Cottage.

CUT LIST
None

HARDWARE AND SUPPLIES (for one pane)
1/8" x 9-15/16" x 14-1/16" clear acrylic plastic pane

1"-diameter wooden cabinet doorknob with mounting screw

4d casing nail

Water sealer

SUGGESTED TOOLS
Layout tools

3/8" drill

1/4" brad-point bit

Orbital sander

INSTRUCTIONS

1. Have a sheet-plastics supplier cut the pane to size. Don't remove the protective paper covering on this pane until you reach Step 4.

2. Locate the center of the window's face by drawing diagonals from its corners. Bore a 1/4" hole through the center, making sure the back face is well supported before you do.

3. Locate and mark a point 1" from an end and centered on the face. Bore a second 1/4" hole through the plastic at this point.

4. Lightly sand the edges and ends of the plastic. Then remove the protective paper coating and install the doorknob in the pane's center hole.

5. Drive a 4d nail into the centered muntin in the window opening, 1" below the top edge of the opening; angle the nail so that the windowpane can be suspended from it without dropping off.

6. To protect the wooden knob, finish it with water sealer.

7. For permanent installation where the weather is typically damp or windy, bore a second hole at the other end of the windowpane and substitute two round-head screws for the one nail.

Mailbox

Send your kids a card for their very own mailbox!

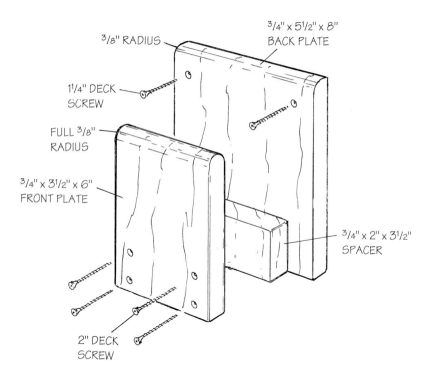

3/8" RADIUS

3/4" x 5½" x 8"
BACK PLATE

1¼" DECK
SCREW

FULL 3/8"
RADIUS

3/4" x 3½" x 6"
FRONT PLATE

3/4" x 2" x 3½"
SPACER

2" DECK
SCREW

CUT LIST

1	3/4" x 5-1/2" x 8"	Back plate
1	3/4" x 3-1/2" x 6"	Front plate
1	3/4" x 3-1/2" x 2"	Spacer

HARDWARE AND SUPPLIES

1-1/4 deck screws (2)
2" deck screws (4)
Exterior alkyd primer
Alkyd enamel paint
Mineral spirits

SUGGESTED TOOLS

Layout tools
No. 2 screwdriver
Circular saw
3/8" drill
Pilot bits to match screw sizes
No. 2 drive bit
Router
3/8" rounding-over bit
Orbital sander
1/2" and 1-1/2" paintbrushes

INSTRUCTIONS

1. Lay out and cut the three parts to length.

2. Using your router with a 3/8" rounding-over bit, round one arris along one end of the back plate and both arrises along one end of the front plate.

3. Sand the three parts well and wipe off the sanding dust when you're through.

4. Stack the three pieces on your work surface, with the back plate on the bottom, the front plate on top, and the spacer in between. Be sure the rounded arris of the back plate faces up, the square edges of all three pieces are flush, and both the front plate and spacer are centered in relation to the width of the back plate. When the pieces are aligned correctly, clamp the stack securely to your work surface.

5. Bore four pilot holes for 2" screws through the face of the top plate and down through the stack. Locate these holes in a rectangular pattern, as shown in the illustration. Also bore two pilot holes for the 1-1/4" mounting screws; locate these holes in the back plate's upper corners, 1" from the end and 1" from each edge.

6. Fasten the three pieces together with four 2" screws driven through the pilot-bored holes.

7. Prime and paint the mailbox as you wish, using exterior-grade finishes. A numbered address or child's name is a nice touch.

8. Mount the mailbox to the plywood front of the Cozy Cottage with two 1-1/4" screws, driving them through the face of the back plate and into the plywood. Make sure your mailbox is mounted low enough for your youngster's height!

RING TOSS

The ancient game of ring toss—known in some locales as *quoits*—has been a worldwide favorite for centuries. This version features knock-down construction and requires a minimum of storage space.

CUT LIST
2	1-1/2" x 1-1/2" x 36"	Bases (A and B)
2	3/4" x 12" dowel	Front posts
1	3/4" x 18" dowel	Center post
2	3/4" x 24" dowel	Rear posts
4	3/16" x 3/4" x 40"	Rings

HARDWARE AND SUPPLIES
1-1/2" deck screws (5)
Resin glue
Heavy waxed thread
Exterior alkyd primer
Alkyd enamel paint
Mineral spirits

SUGGESTED TOOLS
Layout tools
Backsaw
Coping saw
Round rasp
Flat rasp
Chisel
Bench mallet
Pocketknife
No. 2 screwdriver
Circular saw with carbide-tipped blade and rip fence
3/8" drill
3/4" brad-point bit and stop collar
Pilot bit to match screw size
No. 2 drive bit
Orbital sander
1" and 2" paintbrushes
Tub filled with warm water

TIP
■ To make the rings, select a limber, straight-grained wood such as straight-grained pine.

Games & Building Sets

INSTRUCTIONS

1. Cut the base A and base B pieces to length. Next, lay out their centered half-lap joints, which are 1-1/2" long and 3/4" deep. Use a backsaw and a coping saw to cut the half-lap joints. Then test-fit the joint for a comfortable fit. If necessary, trim the cutouts with your chisel.

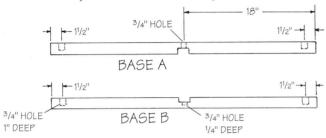

2. Set the two assembled base pieces on some scrap wood on a flat surface, with base A on the bottom. With the pilot bit, bore a centered hole, exactly 1-1/2" from each end of each base piece; also bore a centered hole in the top face of the half-lap joint.

3. Flip the assembly over so that base A is on top and refer to the illustrations. Using the brad-point bit with a stop collar set at 1", bore five 3/4" holes in the same locations as in Step 2.

RING TOSS

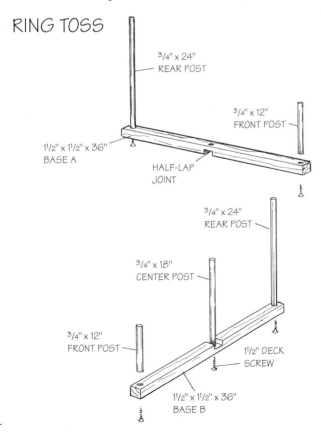

4. Disassemble the base pieces and use a round rasp to remove some material from the center bore hole in base A. Check to see that a 3/4" dowel will slide easily through it. Then reassemble the base pieces.

5. With your backsaw, cut the five dowel posts to length. Using the illustration as a guide, glue one 12" post and one 24" post into the outer holes in each base piece.

6. Take the assembly apart again and carefully turn base A on its side. Using the drive bit, drive a deck screw through each pilot hole into the end of each dowel. Repeat to secure the other two posts in base B. Glue the center post into base B and secure it in position with a deck screw.

7. Use a flat rasp to ease the ends of each post. Then reassemble the base pieces.

8. To rip the 40"-long ring pieces, use a sharp carbide-tipped blade and a rip-fence attachment. (If you own a table saw, so much the better.) For best results, secure your lumber carefully. You may want to rip an extra piece or two to have on hand should you break one during the bending process described in Step 11.

9. Using your coping saw, cut four 1/16"-deep notches on each edge of each ring piece; locate these notches 1/2" and 2-1/2" from each end, for a total of eight notches per piece.

10. Soak the ring pieces in a tub of warm water for about twenty minutes. To keep them submerged, place weights on top of them. Meanwhile, use your pocketknife to cut eight 6"-long pieces of waxed thread.

11. Remove the ring pieces from their bath. Gently work each one into a 12"-diameter circular shape by carefully bending and releasing it a bit at a time so as not to crack the wood. Align the four pairs of notches and use two pieces of thread to secure the ends of each ring tightly together. Set the rings in a shady place to dry.

12. Sand all parts thoroughly and wipe them clean. Then prime and paint the Ring Toss set in any colors you choose. Before the kids start to play, have them assign a point score to the front, center, and back posts. Also, establish a ring-tossing line that's at an appropriate distance for your young players' skill levels.

FOLD-AWAY HOPSCOTCH

Bad weather drives kids indoors, but, inside or out, your children will keep right on hopping with this portable version of an ancient game.

CUT LIST
19 3/8" x 12" Dowels
 2 3/8" x 18" Dowels
 5 3/8" x 24" Dowels

HARDWARE AND SUPPLIES
Screw eyes; wire size 13 (66)
Beeswax candle stub
Exterior alkyd primer
Alkyd enamel paint
Mineral spirits

SUGGESTED TOOLS
Coping saw (or backsaw and miter box)
Twist drill
1/16" twist-drill bit
Slip-joint pliers
Needle-nose pliers
1/2" paintbrush

TIP
■ 5/16" or 1/2" dowels will work just as well as 3/8" dowels.

FOLD-AWAY
HOPSCOTCH

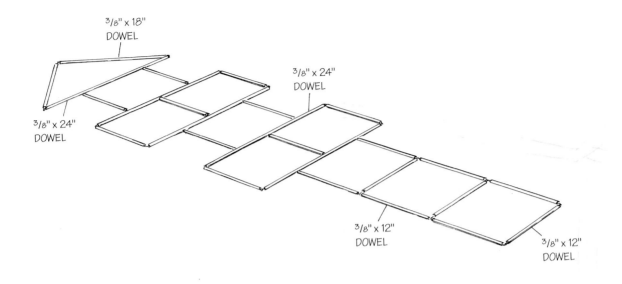

³/₈" x 18" DOWEL

³/₈" x 24" DOWEL

³/₈" x 24" DOWEL

³/₈" x 12" DOWEL

³/₈" x 12" DOWEL

INSTRUCTIONS

1. Lay out and cut the dowels to the lengths listed in the Cut List. (For this purpose, a miter box and backsaw will work even better than a coping saw.)

2. Secure a dowel upright on your work surface. Use your twist drill and 1/16" bit to bore a centered hole, 5/8" deep, into the end of the dowel. Repeat at both ends of every dowel.

3. Lay out and bore two additional holes through each 24" dowel; each hole should be 6" from an end, and each pair of holes should be aligned so that the holes pass through the dowel in the same direction. In four of the five 24" dowels, also bore a hole 12" from either end; be sure to align this hole with the other two holes that pass through each of these dowel's rounded edges.

4. Sand the dowel ends lightly and remove the sawdust with a tack rag.

5. Prime the dowels with exterior alkyd primer and let them dry thoroughly.

6. Arrange the dowels on the floor or ground as shown in the illustration. Then, propping the dowels up slightly with bits of scrap wood, paint them with two coats of any colors you like. Let each coat dry thoroughly.

7. Using a pair of slip-joint pliers, insert a screw eye into each bored hole. To make this job easier, rub a bit of beeswax onto the threads of each screw eye before you begin.

8. To assemble the Fold-Away Hopscotch game, first pry open each screw eye slightly with your needle-nose pliers. Then hook the sets of screw eyes together. Before you retighten the eyes, align each assembled set of screw eyes so that the game will fold up accordion-style. This may take a bit of experimentation, but trust us, it can be done! Finally, squeeze the screw eyes closed again.

CONNECTOR DETAIL

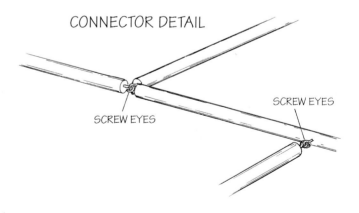

SCREW EYES

SCREW EYES

9. Show your kids how to fold the game into a neat bundle and let them know that this project should be stored indoors when playtime is over.

LIMBER STICK

Here's a simple version of the game that sent the limbo sensation around the world. The Limber Stick's height is easily adjusted by kids and can be positioned high enough for adults to play, too. This project practically begs for a party; put on some loose music (and some loose-fitting clothes) and see how low you can go!

CUT LIST

2 1-1/2" x 1-1/2" x 60"   Standards
2 1-1/2" x 1-1/2" x 1-1/2"   Support handles
4 18" x 5-3/4" x 3/4" plywood Bases A and B
                                  (two pairs)
2 3/8" x 4" dowel   Supports
1 1-1/4" x 54" closet-rod dowel Limber stick

HARDWARE AND SUPPLIES

1-1/2" deck screws (6)
1" deck screws (2)
Resin glue
Exterior alkyd primer
Alkyd enamel paint
   (or exterior-grade polyurethane finish)
Mineral spirits

SUGGESTED TOOLS

Layout tools
Half-round rasp
Coping saw
Panel saw
No. 2 screwdriver
Compass
Circular saw with carbide-tipped blade
3/8" drill
3/8" brad-point bit and stop collar
Pilot bits to match screw sizes
No. 2 drive bit
Orbital sander
1-1/2" paintbrush (or wiping rag)

TIPS

- By all means, use scrap wood for the support handles and pressure-treated solid wood instead of plywood for the bases. Any lightweight wood can be used for the limber stick, but avoid heavy woods such as birch.
- If you can't find 1"-long deck screws, use any exterior screws.
- Always position the stick and its supports so that they face away from the approaching players, or the standards will be knocked over when the stick is bumped.

INSTRUCTIONS

1. Lay out and cut the two standards and the two support handles from the 1-1/2" x 1-1/2" stock, but first read the next step.

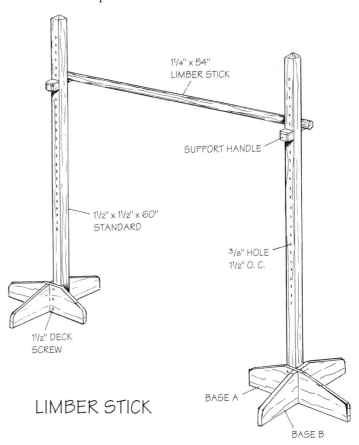

LIMBER STICK

2. There are two ways to shape the ends of the standards and support handles: by using your rasp or by chamfering them with your circular saw. If you use a saw, do this job before you cut the pieces to length so that you'll have plenty of stock for safe sawing. Lay out squared lines, 3/4" from the end on all four sides of both standards and 3/8" from the end on all four sides of both support handles. Set the saw for 45° cutting and turn each piece four times to make the four cuts. Finally, saw the pieces to length.

3. Place a standard face up on your work surface. Set your adjustable square for 3/4". Then use it and a pencil to mark a line all the way down the center of the top face. Mark a centerline down the other standard, too.

4. Measuring along these lines (from the pointed end of each standard), mark each line at 4" and then at every 1-1/2" thereafter (at 5-1/2", 7", and so on) until you've reached 41-1/2". Note that these holes are marked on the illustration as 1-1/2" *O.C.* (or 1-1/2" *on center*). This means that the holes are centered 1-1/2" apart.

5. With your drill and the 3/8" brad-point bit, bore through the marks on both standards. Then set the standards aside.

6. Secure a support handle to your work surface. First find the center of the end opposite to the chamfered end; this can be done by marking two diagonal lines, from corner to corner, across the flat end. Now set the stop collar at 3/4" and bore straight into the center with your drill and 3/8" bit. Repeat with the second support handle.

7. Using the illustration as a guide, lay out the four

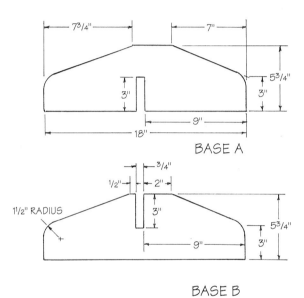

BASE A

BASE B

base pieces A and B on the plywood. Note that the slots on each are 3/4" wide. Then use your circular saw to cut the pieces out.

8. With a panel saw, cut along the 3"-long cutout lines on each piece. With a coping saw, cut out the tabs. Then round the two corners of each base piece. (To make these curved cuts easier, mark a radius for each one, using either a compass set for a 1-1/2" radius or a pencil and any handy container with a round bottom that's 3" in diameter.)

9. Use your panel saw to cut the limber stick to length. (The length can vary, but don't cut the stick so long that it tends to sag in the middle when it's supported at both ends.)

10. Secure the stick to your work surface and chamfer the stick's ends with your rasp.

11. With your panel saw, cut two 4" supports from the 3/8" dowel.

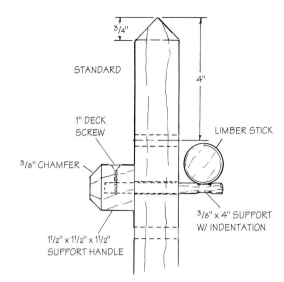

12. Glue each support into the hole in each support handle.

13. Secure a support handle face up on your work surface. Bore a pilot hole for a 1" screw through the face and into the inserted dowel. Then drive a 1" deck screw into the pilot hole. Repeat with the second support handle.

14. With the curved edge of your half-round rasp, shape a concave groove all the way around each support by removing some wood 3/4" from its end. This groove will steady the limber stick when it rests on the supports. Test-fit the supports in the standard holes; if they stick, sand them lightly until they slip in and out easily.

15. Sand all parts thoroughly and remove the sanding dust with a tack rag.

16. To make it easier to match standard holes when you're leveling the limber stick, you may want to stamp or paint matching pairs of letters or numbers next to each matching pair of holes.

17. Attach each standard to a base A piece. First, position a standard and base face to face so that one edge of the standard is aligned with one edge of the slot in the base. Then drive three equally spaced, pilot-bored 1-1/2" deck screws through the base, 3/4" from one edge of the slot and into the standard. Repeat to attach the other standard to the other base A. (Note that the base B pieces are not permanently attached to the assemblies; this allows the project parts to be disassembled for convenient storage in a closet or under a bed.)

18. Finish your Limber Stick project in any way you wish, but pay particular attention to the dowel parts, which aren't pressure-treated for protection against the elements. All our project parts except for the stick itself were clear-coated with an exterior polyurethane finish; the stick was painted in eye-catching colors. Assemble the parts and you're ready to limbo!

Design and build your own monster blocks by starting with this set of plans for a square block. The large grab-holes in each block encourage hours of lively stacking play.

CUT LIST (for one block A only)

2	1/2" x 12" x 12" plywood	Top and bottom
2	1/2" x 11" x 12" plywood	Front and back
2	1/2" x 11" x 11" plywood	Sides
4	1-1/2" x 1-1/2" x 11"	Battens
4	1-1/2" x 1-1/2" x 8"	Battens

HARDWARE AND SUPPLIES

1-3/4" deck screws (36)
Exterior alkyd primer
Alkyd enamel paint
Mineral spirits

SUGGESTED TOOLS

Layout tools
No. 2 screwdriver
Circular saw with carbide-tipped
   and plywood blades
3/8" drill
2" Forstner bit
Pilot bit to match screw size
No. 2 drive bit
Router
3/8" rounding-over bit
Orbital sander
2" paintbrush

TIPS

- The instructions that follow are for block A construction only. Each block, however, no matter what its shape, is assembled from 1/2"-thick plywood pieces and secured by 1-1/2" x 1-1/2" battens. To calculate how much lumber you'll need to make all the shapes, refer both to the illustrations and to the sample Cut List provided for block A.
- Keep in mind that the triangular blocks will require some bevel cuts.

INSTRUCTIONS

1. Using your layout tools and a circular saw fitted with the appropriate blade, lay out the parts and cut them to size. Select the best-looking faces of each piece and, as you assemble the block, position these to face outward.

2. Using a Forstner bit, bore a single 2" hole through the center of each plywood piece.

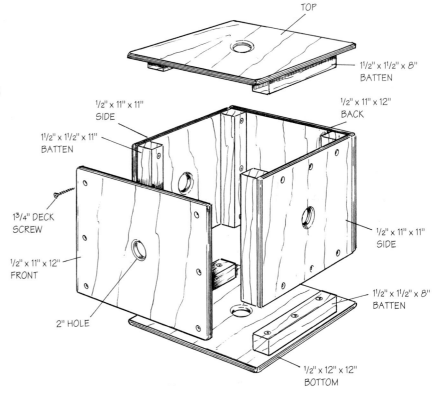

BLOCK A DETAIL

3. Through one face of an 11" batten, bore three pilot holes, spaced 4" apart and centered along the batten's length. Then use 1-3/4" deck screws to fasten the batten to the inside face of a side piece; one edge of the batten should be flush with an edge of the side piece, and its ends should be flush with the side piece's adjacent edges. Repeat to bore and fasten another 11" batten to the same face of the side piece, flush with its opposite edge.

4. Repeat Step 3 to fasten two 11" battens to the other side piece.

5. Bore three equally spaced pilot holes through the face of the front piece, 1-1/4" from an 11" edge. The holes should be 4-1/2" apart. Repeat this pilot-hole pattern along the opposite edge on the same face. Then repeat this entire step to bore six holes in the back piece.

6. Begin the assembly process by butting the battened edge of a side piece against the 11" inside face of the front piece; be sure the edge of the front piece is flush with the outside face of the side piece. Fasten the two pieces with three deck screws, inserting these through the pilot-bored holes in the front piece. Fasten the other side piece to the front piece in the same manner.

7. Use six screws to fasten the back piece onto the remaining two side battens to form an open box shape.

8. Using your router and a 3/8" rounding-over bit, round the inside arris of the 2" holes on the top and bottom pieces.

9. Secure an 8" batten to the inside face of a top piece, but this time position the batten so that one of its edges is 1/2" from one edge of the top piece and each of its ends is 1-1/2" from the top piece's adjacent edges. Secure another batten at the opposite edge of the top piece. Repeat to fasten the last two battens to the bottom piece in the same manner.

10. Using a good-grade exterior alkyd primer, prime the interior of the assembly and the inside surfaces of the top and bottom pieces.

11. Position the top piece so that its battens fit into the open top of the assembled box. Then bore three equally spaced pilot holes through the face of the side piece, 1-1/4" down from the face of the top piece and into the batten behind. The middle hole is centered along the edge, and the other two holes are 3-1/2" to either side of the first one. Repeat to bore three identical pilot holes near the top edge of the opposite side piece. Then fasten the top with six screws. Flip the assembly over and close the cube by boring and fastening together the sides and bottom.

12. Use your router to round the arrises on the outside of the block.

13. Sand the cube thoroughly, paying particular attention to the surfaces around the 2" holes. Dust off the sanding debris, prime the block's exterior, and then paint it as you wish. Let each coat of paint dry well.

BIG BLOCKS

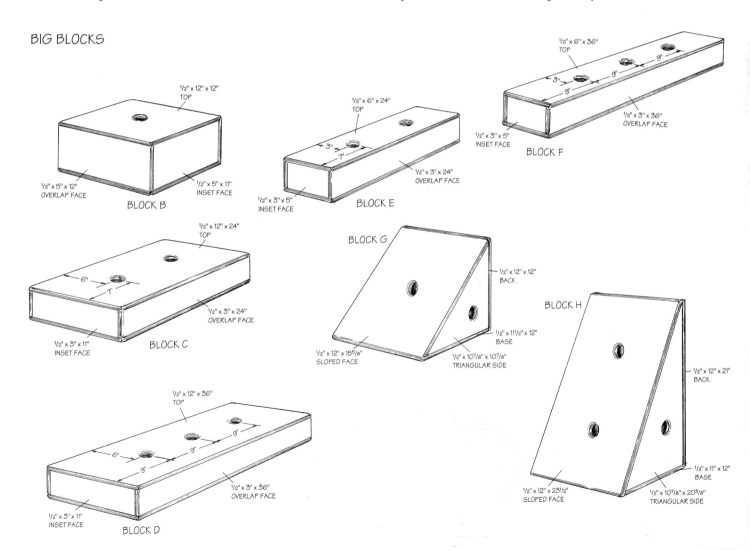

ADVENTURE SET

With its many large-scale parts, this gigantic stacking set encourages play that's both cooperative and imaginative. Feel free to enlarge or reduce the materials list to suit your kids' play needs, but first examine the instructions and illustrations to familiarize yourself with how the parts are assembled and to determine what you'll need.

CUT LIST

10	6" x 6" x 6"	Small timbers
5	6" x 6" x 16"	Medium timbers
15	6" x 6" x 36"	Long timbers
75	1-1/4" x 6-1/2" dowel	Connector posts
75	3/4" x 3-1/2" x 3-1/2"	Connector blocks
75	3/8" x 3" dowel	Connector pins
4	1-1/4" x 48" dowel	Poles
2	3/4" x 16" x 36" plywood	Small panels
2	3/4" x 36" x 36" plywood	Large panels

HARDWARE AND SUPPLIES

36" x 48" ripstop nylon; large tarps (2)
24" x 36" ripstop nylon; small tarps (2)
1/2" x 36" nylon; short ropes (3)
1/2" x 48" nylon; medium ropes (3)
1/2" x 72" nylon; long ropes (3)
1/4" x 12" nylon; ties (16)
1/4" x 48" nylon; ties (6)
3/8" grommets (20)
Water sealer
Kitchen matches
Resin glue

SUGGESTED TOOLS

Layout tools
Panel saw
Backsaw
Pocketknife (or utility knife)
Sharp scissors
Grommet setter with anvil
Circular saw
3/8" drill
1-3/8" Forstner bit
5/16" brad-point bit
3/8" brad-point bit
1/2" reversible drill
1-3/8" self-feeding bit and bit extension
Orbital sander

TIPS

- 6" x 6" rough-sawed cedar is an ideal wood for the timbers. All the dowel parts (except for the poles) may be made of softwoods; the poles should be made of a stronger wood such as birch.
- A crafts-supply dealer is a good source for a grommet setter. See page 65 for instructions on setting grommets.
- Heavy-duty reversible drills are often available at rental shops. Using your 3/8" drill to bore the many 1-3/8" holes in the timber pieces is not recommended. You'll probably have to purchase or borrow the bit and bit extension.

INSTRUCTIONS

1. Using your layout tools and circular saw, cut the three sizes of timbers to length; there are thirty timbers in this set. Unless your saw's blade depth extends to at least 3", you'll have to flip the timber stock four times, saw across each face, and then cut the remaining wood with your panel saw.

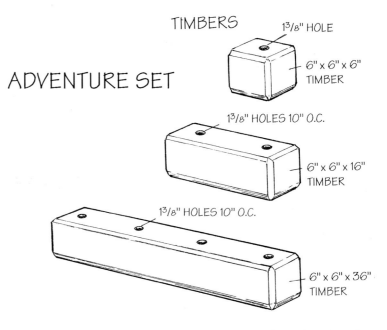

ADVENTURE SET

TIMBERS · 1³/8" HOLE · 6" x 6" x 6" TIMBER · 1³/8" HOLES 10" O.C. · 6" x 6" x 16" TIMBER · 1³/8" HOLES 10" O.C. · 6" x 6" x 36" TIMBER

2. Bore 1-3/8" holes through the face of each timber piece as indicated in the illustration. The 1/2" drill and bit extension will give you the power and reach to bore straight through, and the self-feeding bit will make an otherwise onerous job easy.

3. Set a timber on your work surface. Using an adjustable square set to 5/8", mark lines along the timber's faces

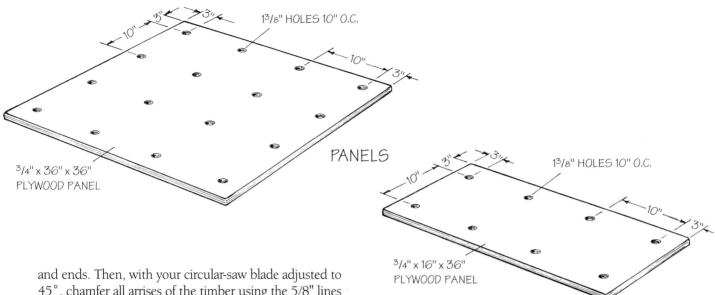

PANELS

$3/4" \times 36" \times 36"$
PLYWOOD PANEL

$1^3/8"$ HOLES 10" O.C.

$1^3/8"$ HOLES 10" O.C.

$3/4" \times 16" \times 36"$
PLYWOOD PANEL

and ends. Then, with your circular-saw blade adjusted to 45°, chamfer all arrises of the timber using the 5/8" lines as guides. Repeat to chamfer all arrises on all the timbers. Then rough-sand the timbers in order to remove large splinters, but leave their coarse texture intact.

4. Lay out the rectangular Panel shapes on plywood and saw them out. Then, using the Illustrations as guides, lay out the patterns for boring and bore the 1-3/8" holes with a Forstner bit. Sand the panels thoroughly.

5. The connector assemblies consist of three pieces: posts, blocks, and pins. Begin by using your backsaw (and a miter box if you have one) to cut the dowel posts and pins to length. Then cut the square blocks to length, too.

8. Slide a post through the hole in a block until the post is centered. Secure the block with one edge up. Locate the center of the top edge (1-3/4" from an end and 3/8" from either face) and, using your drill and a 3/8" brad-point bit, bore a 3"-deep hole into the assembly at that point. This hole should go right through the inserted post.

9. Place a few drops of glue in the bore hole and drive a pin into it. Repeat Steps 7 and 8 to lay out and bore all the connector assemblies. Glue each pin in place. When the glue has dried, sand the assemblies carefully and set them aside.

10. Lay out the poles. Use your backsaw to cut them to length.

CONNECTOR

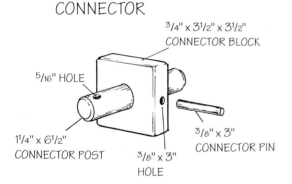

$3/4" \times 3^1/2" \times 3^1/2"$
CONNECTOR BLOCK

$5/16"$ HOLE

$1^1/4" \times 6^1/2"$
CONNECTOR POST

$3/8" \times 3"$
HOLE

$3/8" \times 3"$
CONNECTOR PIN

POLES

$5/16"$ HOLES 11" O. C.

$1^1/4" \times 48"$ POLE

6. Secure a post in a vertical position and make a mark on the rounded side, 1" down from the top end. Bore a 5/16" hole through the post at that point. Repeat to bore identical holes in the other posts.

7. Secure a block face up and locate the center of that face by drawing diagonals corner-to-corner. Bore a 1-3/8" hole through the center mark. Repeat to bore holes through all the blocks.

11. Secure a pole on your work surface for boring. Locate and mark the 24" center point. Also make four more marks, two on each side of the center mark, spacing them 11" apart.

12. Bore a 5/16" hole through each of the five marks. Repeat to lay out and bore the other three poles. Then sand the poles well.

13. Using sharp scissors, cut the four nylon tarps to size. With a grommet setter, place a grommet at each corner of each tarp, leaving at least 1/2" between each grommet's edges and the fabric's edges. Also place a grommet halfway down each long side of the large tarps, with its edge 1/2" from the edge of the tarp.

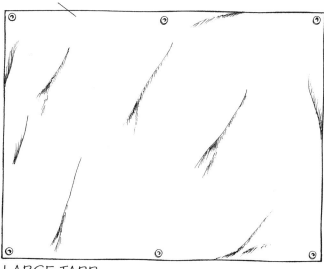

36" x 48"

LARGE TARP

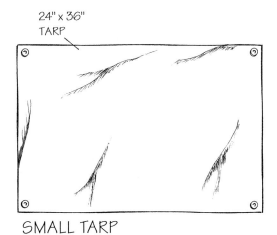

24" x 36"
TARP

SMALL TARP

14. Use a pocketknife or utility knife to cut the ropes and ties to length. To keep the ropes from unraveling, melt their ends slightly with a lit kitchen match.

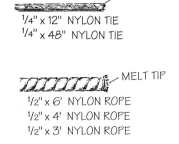

MELT TIP
1/4" x 12" NYLON TIE
1/4" x 48" NYLON TIE

MELT TIP
1/2" x 6' NYLON ROPE
1/2" x 4' NYLON ROPE
1/2" x 3' NYLON ROPE

15. Dust off all the wooden parts and seal them with two coats of water sealer; let the coats dry thoroughly between applications.

16. Assembling the Adventure Set for the first time is a good opportunity to guide your kids and their friends toward some of the building options the various parts offer. Stacking the timbers and panels with connectors between them is easy when it's a group effort. Poles are added to provide masts or antennae, and the ties secure the tarps as sails, as sun shades, or as privacy screens. Have fun!

A World of Play

PLANTER BOX

Kids love gardening. Enough said!

CUT LIST
2   1-1/2" x 9-1/4" x 17"   Ends
2   3/4" x 5-1/2" x 30"   Sides
3   3/4" x 5-1/2" x 26-7/8"   Flooring slats
2   3/4" x 3/4" x 17"   Battens

HARDWARE AND SUPPLIES
1-1/2" deck screws (20)

SUGGESTED TOOLS
Layout tools
No. 2 screwdriver
Circular saw
Jigsaw
3/8" drill
2" Forstner bit
Pilot bit to match screw size
No. 2 drive bit
Router
3/8" rounding-over bit
Orbital sander

TIP
■ If you don't own a 2" Forstner bit, use a jigsaw to cut the holes and semicircular cutouts in the end pieces. You'll then need a drill bit of a size large enough to bore "starter" holes for the jigsaw blade.

INSTRUCTIONS

1. Using your layout tools and circular saw, cut the ends, sides, and flooring slats to length. Then rip the batten stock and cut two battens to length.

2. Secure an end piece face up for boring. As shown in the End Detail, lay out and bore a 1"-radius hole, centered 8-1/2" from one end and 2" from one edge. Bore identical holes in the other end piece.

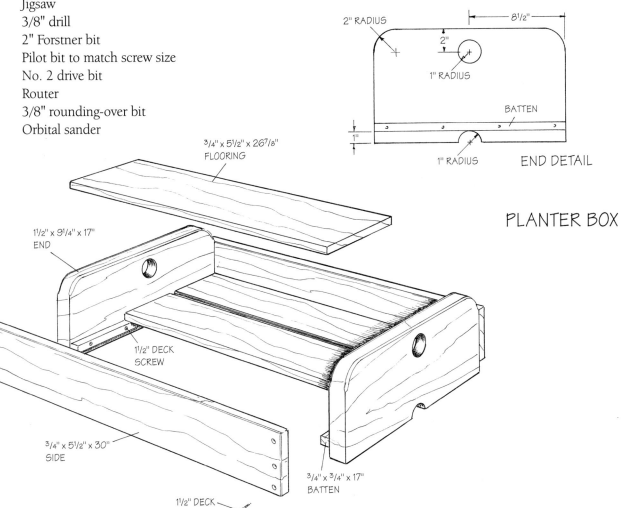

END DETAIL

PLANTER BOX

3. To lay out the semicircles on the two end pieces, butt the bottom edges of the two pieces tightly together on top of some scrap wood and secure the pieces with clamps. Lay out a 2"-diameter circle, centering it along the length of the joint; the circle should be divided in half by the joint line.

4. While the pieces are still firmly butted together, use a 2" Forstner bit to bore out the hole. When you're through, each piece will have a semicircle cut into its bottom edge.

5. Lay out a 2" radius on each upper corner of both end pieces. Cut these radii with your jigsaw.

6. Use your router and 3/8" rounding-over bit to round the arrises on the top edges of both end pieces. Stop routing at the end of each radius.

7. Secure a side piece face up, with plenty of scrap wood beneath it. Rout all four upper arrises. Also rout both arrises of the hole and semicircular cutout. Repeat on the other side piece.

8. Use your layout tools and a drill chucked with the pilot bit to bore three pilot holes, spaced 2-1/4" apart, 3/4" from an end of one side piece. Repeat to bore three pilot holes near the other end of the side piece and near

both ends of the second side piece.

9. Secure a batten face up. Lay out and bore four equally spaced pilot holes centered along the batten's face. The holes nearest each end should be 3/4" from the ends. Repeat to bore the other batten.

10. Sand all parts thoroughly and remove the sanding debris with a tack rag.

11. Begin assembly by using four deck screws to fasten a batten to the inside face of an end piece, parallel to and 1" from the end piece's bottom edge. Repeat to fasten a batten to the other end piece.

12. Set the end pieces on end, spacing their outer faces 30" apart. Place a side piece on top. Align its ends flush with the outside arrises of the end pieces and align one of its edges 1" above the end piece's square corners. Drive six deck screws to fasten the side down. Repeat to fasten the other side piece.

13. Place the flooring slats in the assembly so that they span the battens to form a bottom for the planter box; leave 1/4" spaces between the center slat and the slats on either side of it. Help your young gardener fill the box, plant seeds, and maintain the garden!

Sized for growing hands, this sturdy three-piece tool set will delight young gardeners.

CUT LIST

Hoe

1	1" x 35" dowel	Handle
1	3/4" x 4" x 4"	Hoe head

Shovel

1	1" x 31" dowel	Handle
2	3/4" x 3-1/2" x 8"	Shovel halves

Rake

1	1" x 34-1/2" dowel	Handle
1	1-1/2" x 1-1/2" x 9"	Rake head
1	1/4" x 8" x 8" plywood	Support
10	3/8" x 2-3/4" dowel	Teeth

HARDWARE AND SUPPLIES

Hoe: 1-1/2" deck screw (1)

Shovel: 1-1/2" deck screws (5)

Rake: 1-1/4" deck screw (1)
1" deck screws (5)
Resin glue

All: Exterior-grade varnish (or exterior alkyd primer and alkyd enamel paint)

SUGGESTED TOOLS

Layout tools
Compass
Backsaw
Coping saw
Block plane
No. 2 screwdriver
Flat rasp
Circular saw
Jigsaw
3/8" drill
3/8" brad-point bit
1" brad-point bit
Pilot bits to match screw sizes
Orbital sander

INSTRUCTIONS

1. Lay out, cut, and assemble the three tools individually. Beginning with the hoe, first use your backsaw to cut the dowel handle to 35" in length.

2. Using the illustrations as guides, cut the 3/4" x 4" x 4" hoe head to size. Then secure it with one long edge facing up and bevel that long edge with your block plane to form a "cutting" edge.

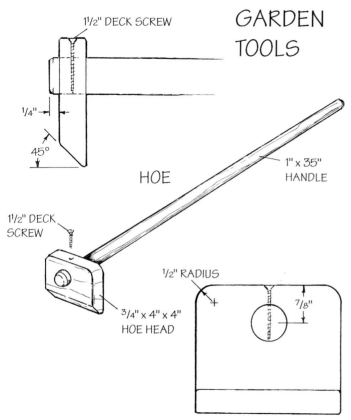

GARDEN TOOLS

HOE

1½" DECK SCREW

1/4"

45°

1" x 35" HANDLE

1½" DECK SCREW

¾" x 4" x 4" HOE HEAD

½" RADIUS

7/8"

3. Use a compass to lay out two 1/2" radii on the square corners, marking them on the face. Cut the radii with your jigsaw.

4. With the hoe head secured face up for drilling, lay out and bore a 1"-diameter hole, centered 7/8" from the edge opposite the beveled edge.

5. Slide the handle through the head's bore hole so that one end protrudes by 1/4". The bevel on the head should face toward the 1/4" protrusion. Now, to secure the parts together, drive a 1-1/2" deck screw through the edge opposite the bevel so that it pierces the handle.

6. With a rasp, chamfer the handle's end just enough to make it comfortable for small hands. Then sand the hoe well.

7. To make the shovel, first saw its dowel handle to 31" in length. Then secure the handle and use your block plane to bevel one end to form a 2"-long "flat." The end of the handle should be beveled to about 1/2", but the exact shape and depth of the bevel aren't critical.

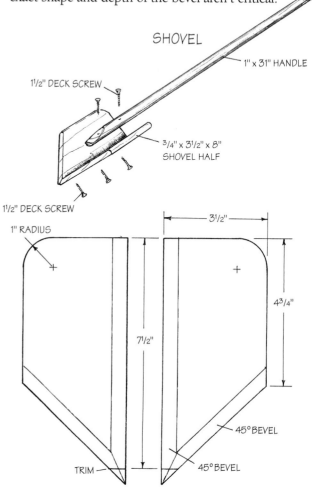

SHOVEL

1" x 31" HANDLE

1½" DECK SCREW

¾" x 3½" x 8" SHOVEL HALF

1½" DECK SCREW

1" RADIUS

3½"

4¾"

7½"

45° BEVEL

45° BEVEL

TRIM

8. The two shovel halves are cut as mirror images of each other so that they'll fit together to make a V-shape. Referring to the Shovel illustrations, lay out one shovel half on a piece of 3/4" stock. To avoid injury, secure the piece well before you cut it!

9. Saw the two 45° bevels as shown. Then use your jigsaw to cut out the piece, including the 1" radius on the shovel's "heel." Repeat Step 8 and this step with the second shovel piece but remember to lay this piece out in reverse.

10. Secure a shovel half with the bevels facing down. Then, through the face, bore three pilot holes for 1-1/2" screws. Locate these holes 1/2" from the bevel's outer edge and 3" apart, lining them up so that they "split" the long bevel.

11. You may need a hand with this step. Secure the hole-free shovel piece with its long bevel up. Then align the long bevel of the bored shovel piece with the bevel of the first. Now drive three 1-1/2" deck screws into the three pilot holes, tightening the bevels together to form the V-shape of the shovel.

12. Secure the shovel assembly with the pointed end on top. Use your backsaw to trim the sharp tip so as to form a bevel of approximately 45°. (The bevel needn't be exact.)

13. Secure the dowel handle for boring, with the beveled "flat" facing up. Through the dowel's thickness, bore pilot holes for two 1-1/2" screws; bore the first hole 1" from the beveled end, right through the "flat," and the second hole 4" from the same end, straight through the dowel.

14. Chamfer the handle's end and sand both pieces well.

15. Place 4" of the beveled end of the handle into the V of the shovel. Fasten the two pieces together with two 1-1/2" screws driven through the handle's pilot holes and into the joint of the two shovel halves.

16. To build the rake, first cut the 1" dowel handle to 34-1/2" in length. Chamfer one end of the handle with your rasp.

17. Cut the 9"-long rake head from 1-1/2" x 1-1/2" stock. Set this piece face up and bore a centered, 1"-diameter, 1-1/4"-deep hole into the top face.

18. Flip the rake head a quarter-turn so that the bore hole is now facing you. Then, on the top face, lay out and bore a row of ten equally spaced 3/8" holes, 3/4" deep and centered along the rake head's length.

19. Use your backsaw to cut each of the ten 3/8" dowel teeth to 2-3/4" in length. Then secure each tooth in turn and use your coping saw to trim a 45° bevel on one end. Finally, glue the teeth into the 3/8" holes in the rake head, turning the bevels toward the 1" bore hole.

20. Using the Support Detail as a guide, lay out and cut the triangular support piece from 1/4" plywood; each side should measure 8". Then cut out the triangular shape from one side.

21. Through the support, bore five pilot holes for 1" screws as follows: two through the face of each "leg," spaced 1-1/2" apart and set 1/2" from the edge with the cutout in it; and one centered 3/4" from the point of the triangle.

22. Sand all parts carefully and remove the sanding debris.

23. Glue the handle into the rake head's bore hole. Secure it by inserting a 1-1/4" deck screw through the rake head so that it pierces the handle.

24. Set the rake assembly onto your work surface, with the teeth facing down. Then place the support piece onto the rake head and handle so that the cutout edge lines up with the edge of the rake head farthest from the handle. The support should be exactly centered on the head. Drive five 1" deck screws through the pilot holes and into the rake head and handle.

25. Finish the tools with two coats of exterior-grade materials. Like many outdoor playthings, your youngster's tool set will last for years if it's cleaned and put away when the day's garden chores are done.

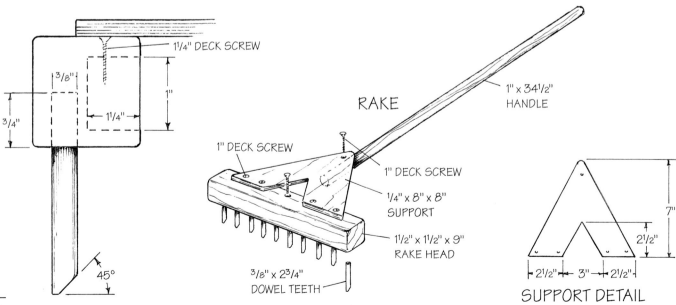

RAKE

1" x 34 1/2" HANDLE

1 1/4" DECK SCREW

3/8"

1"

1 1/4"

3/4"

45°

1" DECK SCREW

1" DECK SCREW

1/4" x 8" x 8" SUPPORT

1 1/2" x 1 1/2" x 9" RAKE HEAD

3/8" x 2 3/4" DOWEL TEETH

7"

2 1/2"

2 1/2"   3"   2 1/2"

SUPPORT DETAIL

Bridges are built for crossing, but children also love them because they're perfect places for visiting with one another and for surveying the world at large. Place the finished project across a flowing rivulet or a small depression in a grassy lawn.

CUT LIST

2	1-1/2" x 5-1/2" x 48"	Supports
3	1-1/2" x 3" x 18-1/2"	Braces
13	1-1/2" x 3-1/2" x 24"	Treads

HARDWARE AND SUPPLIES

2-1/2" deck screws (1 pound)

Exterior-grade polyurethane finish (or water sealer)

SUGGESTED TOOLS

Layout tools

No. 2 screwdriver

Circular saw

Jigsaw

3/8" drill

Pilot bit to match screw size

No. 2 drive bit

Router

3/8" rounding-over bit

Orbital sander

2" paintbrush

INSTRUCTIONS

1. Saw the two supports to length. Position one support face up on your work surface, with one long edge facing you. Then refer to the Support Detail. Lay out one mark on each end, 1" up from the corners nearest to you, and two marks on the nearest edge, 8-1/2" from the same corners. Use your try square to square the marks across the edges and ends. Then, on the arris farthest from you, make a mark exactly 24" from an end.

2. Use your pencil to sketch a broad curve on the face, extending from one 1" mark to the other; the top of the curved line should just intersect the 24" center of the upper arris. Then connect the two 8-1/2" marks in the same manner. The distance between the two lines should be the same throughout.

3. Cut the two curved lines with your jigsaw. Then use the support you've cut as a pattern to scribe and saw out a second support.

4. Using the illustration as a guide, bore six pilot holes through the face of each support. (Note that

the outside pairs of pilot holes are angled 22-1/2° off the vertical.) Set the two supports 18-1/2" apart on a flat surface so that they're resting on their 8-1/2"-long edges.

5. Using your router with 3/8" rounding-over bit, round all the arrises on the two supports except for the curved upper arrises and the 8-1/2"-long arrises.

6. Rip the braces to a 3" width and then cut them to length. Fasten them between the two supports, using deck screws driven through the pilot holes in the supports.

7. Cut the thirteen treads to length. At each end of each one, bore a pair of pilot holes, 2-1/2" apart and 2" from the tread's ends.

8. With your router and rounding-over bit, round the arrises of the treads' ends and those on the upper face of each tread as well.

9. Thoroughly sand the treads and the assembled supports and braces and remove all sanding dust.

10. Set a tread onto the assembly so that it spans the centers of the two supports and extends equally over their edges. To secure the tread, drive four screws into its pilot holes.

11. Using two identical blocks of 1/4"-thick wood as spacers (scraps of lattice work well), secure the remaining treads to the supports, taking care to center each tread across the supports. Work from the center of the supports outward and check now and then with your tape measure to see that the treads don't go astray.

12. To maintain the natural beauty of your footbridge, finish it with a transparent finish such as water sealer or exterior-grade polyurethane.

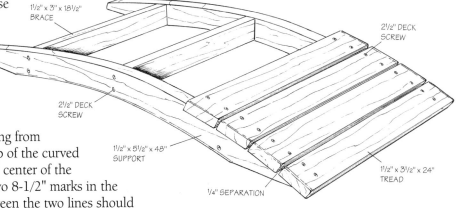

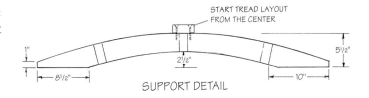

SUPPORT DETAIL

Kids love to examine living things: colorful butterflies and mysterious moths, secretive lizards, and slithery garden snakes. An Observation Station set out on the lawn will help your children to study their finds for a day and then release them to the wild once again. Encourage the kids to provide for the needs of the creatures they discover: sun or shade, a few twigs to crawl about on, leaves for cover, or a bit of water to drink.

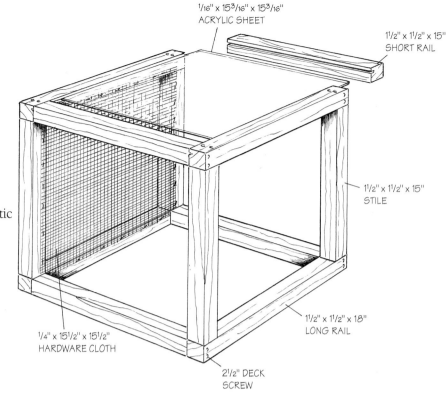

1/16" x 15³/16" x 15³/16" ACRYLIC SHEET

1¹/2" x 1¹/2" x 15" SHORT RAIL

1¹/2" x 1¹/2" x 15" STILE

1¹/2" x 1¹/2" x 18" LONG RAIL

1/4" x 15¹/2" x 15¹/2" HARDWARE CLOTH

2¹/2" DECK SCREW

CUT LIST

4	1-1/2" x 1-1/2" x 18"	Long rails
4	1-1/2" x 1-1/2" x 15"	Short rails
4	1-1/2" x 1-1/2" x 15"	Stiles

HARDWARE AND SUPPLIES

2-1/2" deck screws (32)
1/4"-mesh hardware cloth (36" x 36")
1/8" x 15-3/16" x 15-3/16" acrylic plastic
3/8" staples

SUGGESTED TOOLS

Layout tools
Adjustable square
Tin snips
No. 2 screwdriver
Circular saw with rip fence
3/8" drill
Pilot bit to match screw size
No. 2 drive bit
Staple gun

TIPS

■ All the 1-1/2" x 1-1/2" pieces can be ripped from a single 1-1/2" x 3-1/2" x 8' board. If you choose to do this, you'll need to set your circular saw's rip fence to exactly the same dimension as the lumber's thickness, as actual thicknesses vary slightly from board to board.

■ Have the dealer cut the acrylic to size for you. If it comes with thin protective sheeting on either side, leave the sheeting in place until your project has been completed; it will protect the acrylic against scratches during assembly.

INSTRUCTIONS

1. Use your layout tools and circular saw to cut the long rails, the short rails, and the stiles to length.

2. With an adjustable square set at 1/4", set your circular saw blade to the same depth. Set the rip fence to 1/4" as well.

3. Use your circular saw with rip fence to rip grooves along the edges of two long rails and two short rails; keep the fence tight against the face of each piece as you saw. To ensure that the pieces don't "crawl" as you make these cuts, secure each one in a vise or tack it to the work

surface with a couple of 4d finish nails. Toe-nail these well out of the way of the blade and wear eye protection when you saw—always!

4. Use your 3/8" drill and pilot bit to bore all four long rails as shown in the Long Rail Detail.

LONG RAIL DETAIL

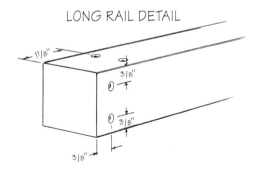

1/8"

3/8"

3/8"

3/8"

5. Before you assemble the project, sand all twelve pieces and then wipe them carefully with a tack rag to remove the sanding debris.

6. On any flat, broad surface, position the grooved long and short rails to form a frame shape. Next, fit the acrylic piece into the 1/4" grooves. Then use your drill and a No. 2 drive bit to secure all four corners of the frame with 2-1/2" deck screws inserted in the pilot-bored holes in the long rails.

7. Assemble a second, bottom frame (without an acrylic panel) with the other long rails and short rails.

8. Complete the framework by using 2-1/2" deck screws to attach the top and bottom frames to the four stiles, once again inserting the screws through the pilot-bored holes.

9. Touch up the frame with sandpaper and wipe it thoroughly with a tack rag.

10. Use your tin snips to cut the hardware cloth into four 15-1/2" x 15-1/2" pieces. Then, from each corner of

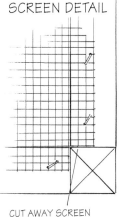

SCREEN DETAIL

CUT AWAY SCREEN
AT EACH CORNER
AS NECESSARY

each piece of cloth, cut away a square piece about 1/4" x 1/4" in size. These cutouts are made to accommodate the corners of the rails when the cloth is fastened in place (see Steps 11 and 12). As you install it, you may find that you need to remove a bit more cloth for a neat fit.

11. Set the assembled frame down on a flat surface so that it rests on one side, with the acrylic piece facing away from your body. Position a piece of hardware cloth inside the frame that rests on the flat surface and fasten the cloth to the stiles and rails with staples.

12. Turn the assembly 90° and repeat Step 11 with another piece of hardware cloth. Continue to turn the frame and fasten squares of cloth to it until all four sides are covered. Weave any loose wire ends into adjoining squares of cloth, trimming any that are too short to weave.

13. Remove the protective sheeting from the acrylic and you're done. Now give your "natural historians" a gift they'll really enjoy!

CHAPTER SEVEN

Designing for Outdoor Play

Designing objects for outdoor play is a uniquely satisfying endeavor because it seeks no other purpose than to exercise growing minds and bodies. This section, included for the many builders who seek the special challenges of designing play projects from the ground up, will give you some idea of how to set up a design space, select tools, and design play equipment that's both fun and useful.

SETTING UP DESIGN SPACE

While moments of inspiration can occur at the workbench, behind the wheel of the family car, or in the bathtub (Eureka!), a strong case can be made for fixing up a corner as an "idea factory." Designing is an art form every bit as important as the building process; as such, it deserves at least a few square feet of uninterrupted floor space.

Because some projects for kids look deceptively simple in the mind's eye, it's easy to get into the habit of dreaming up projects that "feel" great but that won't stand the test for further development—a working plan drawn to scale or (for more complex structures) a scale model. To turn that first flourish of brain cells into a plan or model, there's nothing like having your design space—with an accessible collection of drawing tools—waiting nearby.

Your design environment should be a comfortable place in which you'll enjoy spending bits of unstructured creative time. While it needn't be fancy (and most aren't), any space for design requires a decent work surface, ade-

quate storage space, and proper lighting. For drafting work, a desk or table will suffice in a pinch, but a surface that angles toward you a bit—say 12° or so—will really save strain on your arms. Either a bona fide drafting table with an adjustable work surface or a separate drawing board that can be angled above your worktable will do. These items can be expensive but are often available secondhand and in good condition.

A small cart, shelf unit, or discarded table placed beside your drawing table is useful for storing and organizing both drawing tools that will roll off angled surfaces and the smaller odds and ends that you'll accumulate. Carts on casters are available from office-supply and drafting-supply stores.

Adequate lighting comes in two varieties: area lighting to help you keep track of your various tools and spot lighting for close work. Overhead lighting is fine as long as the light source and your body don't conspire to cast a shadow across your work surface. Hanging lights placed a couple of feet above your table are ideal. Position these carefully so that they don't create a glare. For close work, a lamp with an articulating arm is perfect.

DESIGN TOOLS AND MATERIALS

Design tools begin with the obvious—a sharp pencil or a pen and a sheet of paper. A visit to a drafting-supply store or an art-materials store can be a revelation for the novice designer, and—fair warning—your collection can bulge rapidly. Consider both the probable return on any potential investment and ways to get by with what you already own. That said, there are a few design tools that really make things happen. Among them are the following:

    —Pens and pencils
    —Eraser
    —Craft knife
    —Architect's rule
    —30-60-90-degree triangle
    —T-square
    —Straightedge
    —Flexible curve

To these design tools, you might also add a sharp pair of scissors, a can of spray adhesive (for gluing small, cutout design elements onto your original sketches), and cellophane tape for securing your drawing paper.

FINDING OUT WHAT KIDS WANT

Now that you have some creative space and tools, where's the inspiration? How can you build opportunities for creative problem-solving into a project? By becoming a child yourself.

Easier said than done, of course; everyone knows that bones and brain matter begin to fossilize after one's thirteenth birthday! Letting the child within the adult body step up to the drawing board can be a real challenge.

Following are some suggestions for designing from a child's point of view:

—*Squirm.* A child's mind is a child's body is a child's mind…Just try to pry them apart, if you dare! While you're designing a project, spend some imaginary time inside a child's body clothed in torn jeans, a T-shirt, and a beat-up pair of tennis shoes. Put yourself into the structure you're planning and examine each element from a child's perspective. Are the parts sized appropriately for little hands? Are openings and passageways safe and inviting, and do they lead to further play options? Are there a variety of vantage points in this imaginary structure—to peek through, to spy from, and to reach between? Places from which you can engage the world and its inhabitants in all their terrific complexity?

—*Observe.* Visit backyards, public parks, playgrounds, and schoolyards—anywhere children congregate—and observe children at play. Given a little time, you'll see patterns of invention in their play, ones that will give you design and building clues. Watch them as they discover new avenues of exploration in a play structure: how to get from down here to up there; what to hold onto for security when hanging upside down; and which way to get in, out, around, and back up. Kids solve these problems over and over again in innovative and often hilarious ways. Learn from their experiences.

—*Compare.* Check your suppositions and your observations against established standards of safety, play behavior, age-appropriateness, structural strength, and accessibility. You'll find information on all these subjects at your local library; building for play is a subject of much professional research.

INCLUDING WHAT KIDS NEED

Most people today know that play is more than fun and games—that there's more going on in the busy sandbox than casual observation will reveal. But what is play, actually? What should it be? And what do children most enjoy playing with? Learning more about play behavior can greatly improve your project plans.

What we call *child's play* is actually a complex and fascinating business, one that seems to defy categorization. Most of all, of course, play—and the place where it takes place—should be fun. A place for play should be a place where kids feel at home, where they can stretch their growing bodies in new ways, and where they'll find spots for quiet contemplation as well. A single-use project quickly grows tiresome, so make your structures places that invite invention of all sorts—places where your kids can investigate their own world and the environment around them in healthy ways.

Few single play structures can offer such a complete range of opportunities, but some of them should be included in any structure that you design. The cold, hard reality is that unless the projects you build provide children with these challenges and opportunities, most kids will soon lose interest and seek out more interesting adventures elsewhere. For more information about child development and play, your local library can offer materials for further reading.

Always remember that the real goal of your design efforts should be to foster your children's ever-changing creative activity, just as a hillside covered with surprises might. And the joy on your kids' faces is the only reward that you'll ask for your labors.

METRIC CONVERSION CHARTS

Lengths

Inches	CM	Inches	CM
1/8	0.3	20	50.8
1/4	0.6	21	53.3
3/8	1.0	22	55.9
1/2	1.3	23	58.4
5/8	1.6	24	61.0
3/4	1.9	25	63.5
7/8	2.2	26	66.0
1	2.5	27	68.6
1-1/4	3.2	28	71.1
1-1/2	3.8	29	73.7
1-3/4	4.4	30	76.2
2	5.1	31	78.7
2-1/2	6.4	32	81.3
3	7.6	33	83.8
3-1/2	8.9	34	86.4
4	10.2	35	88.9
4-1/2	11.4	36	91.4
5	12.7	37	94.0
6	15.2	38	96.5
7	17.8	39	99.1
8	20.3	40	101.6
9	22.9	41	104.1
10	25.4	42	106.7
11	27.9	43	109.2
12	30.5	44	111.8
13	33.0	45	114.3
14	35.6	46	116.8
15	38.1	47	119.4
16	40.6	48	121.9
17	43.2	49	124.5
18	45.7	50	127.0
19	48.3		

Volumes

1 fluid ounce	29.6 ml
1 pint	473 ml
1 quart	946 ml
1 gallon (128 fl. oz.)	3.785 l

Weights

0.035 ounces	1 gram
1 ounce	28.35 grams
1 pound	453.6 grams

ACKNOWLEDGEMENTS

▼

I'd like to thank the following people for their generous contributions to Building Outdoor Play Structures:

Anne Kellie McGuire, *psychoeducational therapist, for advice on developmentally appropriate play*
Steve McGuire, *contractor, for technical advice on the projects*
Friends and family *for their enthusiastic support and suggestions and for providing locations for photography*
Evan Bracken (*Light Reflections, Hendersonville, NC*) *for the book's photography*
Don Osby (*Page 1 Publications, Horse Shoe, NC*) *for his illustrations of the projects*
The kids, *who reinvent play everyday*

Our lively models
The Kids

Will and Wesley Albrecht
Evan Boswell
Sara Devin Clark
Mark Eaton deVerges
Carter Haun
Henry and C.J. Hilgendorf
Shaneise and Shaneika Hutchinson
Taemi J. and Elli J. Kim
Sally Virginia and Will Lee
Ashley Logan
Ivan Randolph and Margaret Amelia Mathena
Katie McGalliard
Molly McGuire
Alex Minkin
Sarah Olesiuk
Anthony and Blake Peele
Emily Samsel
Hillary Sherman
Ian Barton Simpson
Mariah Thomas
Chase L. Twilley
Olivia Wallenborn
Charles and William Watkins

The Grownups

John Faherty
Amy Stryker Mathena
Anne McGuire
Zoe Rhine
Cindy Wheeler Lee

The photographs on pages 6 and 98 were taken by the author.